RETAIN OR RETRAIN

How to Keep the Good Ones from Leaving

RETAIN OR RETRAIN

How to Keep the Good Ones from Leaving

Donald Sanders, Ph.D.

Lew Losoncy, Ed.D.   Carol Hacker   Ed Rose

David Cox, Ph.D.   Teri Yanovitch   David Baker, Ph.D.

INSYNC PRESS

Published by InSync Communications LLC, InSync Press
2445 River Tree Circle
Sanford, FL 32771
http://www.insynchronicity.com

This book was set in Trump Medieaval
Cover Design and Composition by Jonathan Pennell

Library of Congress Catalog Number Pending
            Sanders. Donald.,
Retain or Retrain
            ISBN: 1-929902-11-5

First InSync Press Edition
10 9 8 7 6 5 4 3 2 1
Printed in the United States of America

CONTENTS

INTRODUCTION
The Problem and the Solution

OVERVIEW

Most companies have a vague notion that employee retention is a problem. Most managers and supervisors know that, when an employee leaves the company, even though she may have been with that company less than a year, some special knowledge, skills, and customer value leave with her. However, too many companies have a fatalistic attitude about retention and turnover; they think that it is just part of being in business—and, of course some of it is. But most unwanted turnover is both costly and avoidable. In the 1960's and 1970's we accepted the fact that a certain percentage of "defective product" or "flawed service" was just a part of business. In the 1980's, using a new paradigm of continuous improvement and process control, we dramatically reduced defects and poor service—if we hadn't, many more companies would have gone out of business. Retention (or, for the "glass is half empty" crowd, turnover) is the new century's "defective product." It is a problem with a solution, not an acceptable facet of doing business. This book defines the problem and presents a variety of practical solutions.

THE PROBLEM

Imagine, if you will, a typical American company of 1000 employees. It could be a manufacturing company or a service company, it could be a dotcommer or a traditional distribution organization, it could be full of technical specialists or sales reps—it doesn't make any difference.

Now imagine that this company experiences a five percent turnover rate. This really is not that high, it represents only fifty people (one per week) per year out of one thousand. Further imagine that half of these people are "good" turnover; that is, for one reason or another, their leaving either didn't hurt the company or allowed the company to meet some other goals. These are the people with outdated skills, poor performance histories, or positions that were going to be eliminated anyway. So, they don't count against the company's "bad" or "unwanted" turnover. Thus, this fictional company lost 2.5 percent of its workforce or 25 people during the year that it really wanted to keep.

Here's the question. How much did this cost the company?

Need more information? Assume that all were experienced, at least two years with the company. Seven of the twenty-five were administrative support personnel averaging $30,000 per year, five were repair specialists averaging $40,000 per year, three were mid level managers averaging $70,000 per year, three were engineers averaging $75,000 per year, five were information technology staff averaging $75,000 per year, and two were senior level managers whose salary and bonus package was close to $200,000. Now, what was the cost?

Conservatively, **this company watched two million three hundred sixty-five thousand dollars walk out the door.** This is the documentable hard cost of replacing employees in terms of recruiting, interviewing, hiring, and lost productivity during learning curve time. This figure does not include the cost of lost customers, lost sales, lost teamwork etc. In reality, this could easily increase the figure by another 30%. Would the CEO of this company, would the managers of the departments that these people worked in, climb up to the roof of the building and throw two and a half million dollars to the wind? Not likely. Then why would they let this money walk out the door?

Because, for the most part, they believe that it is an unavoidable cost of doing business. But it is not; it most definitely is not. As a matter of fact, turnover is a hidden cost of doing business in most companies. For example, managers in most EVA companies are not typically charged for the unnecessary loss of a good employee. Most Profit and Loss statements don't reflect the cost of turnover. I have never seen NOPAT-AT (Net Operating Profit After Taxes—And Turnover) in a financial statement.

But it is there, and it is a quantifiable cost of business not unlike the cost of producing defective products or providing poor service. Like defective products and poor service, **unwanted turnover is avoidable, and the solution is at once simple and complex**. Yes, one of the easiest ways to increase overall profitability is not to lay people off (how many companies "shrink" their way to success?) but to keep the ones you want from walking away.

Yet this problem, the problem of employee retention, which costs businesses in this country billions of dollars a year, **is systematically approached by less than 50% of the companies in this country**. Turnover is especially rampant among people who have been with the company less than two years in companies with more than 250 employees. And it doesn't have to be. There is a solution.

So, let's look at the solution.

THE SOLUTION

Just pay them more money, right?

Wrong. Believe it or not, turnover is seldom about money, it is about another m—management. Let me clarify this by looking quickly at two myths.

The first myth is that people will switch companies for a dollar an hour, two thousand a year, a better benefits program. And that is what it is, a myth. Certainly there are some companies where good, well-managed employees are leaving a stable firm to join a new e-company with the hope that he or she will become an instant millionaire. Sure there are engineers who are leaving good jobs to become IT specialists at forty to fifty percent increases in income. But these are the exception. When venture capital firms are recruiting investment bankers with the promise of exceedingly large financial rewards, it is a different game. But this is not where the majority of turnover in this country occurs. And the lesson for these companies is that study after study points to the fact that **money is seldom the root cause of turnover**, it is often a contributing cause, but not the root cause. In more than seventy-five percent of turnover, the root cause, the real reason that people leave is how they are treated by the company and/or by their direct supervisor.

Fortune Magazine's cover article of May 29, 2000 provides support for this position. Fortune asked 10 major employers ranging from Cisco to GE, from Enron to Goldman Sachs what they did to reduce turnover. In each of the ten cases money was not the primary strategy for keeping good employees. Rather it was the strategic positioning of management strategies (e.g. career development), employee management (e.g. decision making authority) and good business practices (thorough hiring practices) that made the difference.

Which leads us to the second myth: the myth of the validity of the exit interview. I have been hired by companies with high turnover to conduct exit interviews with people who had exit interviews with their direct supervisor and/or the Human Resource Department. In the interviews with the supervisor and the HR departments, the most frequently cited causes of leaving these companies were (in this order): salary, benefits working conditions, commute/family time conflicts, conflict with immediate supervisor (this came from the HR interviews, obviously).

What about the interviews that I conducted? First, please understand that in my interviews I promised the individual anonymity, the company was looking for trends and solutions, not who caused the individual to leave. Also understand that, because of the promised anonymity those being interviewed understood that I could not negatively affect their career. Most were more than willing to unburden, some were reluctant to share more than a condensed version of why they left and some didn't want to talk at all. The results of these interviews were consistent across companies.

Between sixty and sixty-five percent of the people I interviewed said they left because of issues related to their direct supervisor, for example: not being listened to, not being challenged, no sense of personal development, supervisor style of "my way or the highway," lack of respect, obvious favoritism (particularly in terms of promotional opportunities), no teamwork, rules not applied equally to everyone, no encouragement/praise/recognition, a sense of being ignored or isolated and boring, repetitive work (knowing other types of work were available).

Another fifteen to twenty percent (depending on the company) of the turnover was due to what I term company-wide systemic issues. These included no perceived chance to be promoted, static or declining size, revenue or market share, limited career growth opportunities, no sense of pride in the company or their department, company wide poor promotion practices, a perceived sense of poor management company-wide and unrealistic expectations across the company (for example, everyone was expected to work 60 hour weeks, Saturdays, etc).

And finally, the third group of reasons, ranging anywhere from fifteen to thirty percent in my experience, was in a category called compensation/comfort issues. These included salary, benefits, length of commute, too much travel or time away from home, physical office environment, and regularly abusive customers.

Why were my results so different from those of the direct supervisor or the Human Resources Department? Obviously, if you don't respect your supervisor's style you are not likely to tell this to him or her. People didn't want to "burn bridges," hurt someone's feelings, or get bad references. So, generally they just said, "I got a better offer," or "I needed more money," or "closer to home." But the real reasons had more to do with management than money.

HOW TO REDUCE UNWANTED TURNOVER

Make no mistake about it, then. Most turnover is a management issue. Most turnover is a result of a company-wide, divisional, departmental or individual supervisor treatment of the people who work in the environment created by those in charge. This environment was created and it can be changed. Like any change effort, it takes conscious effort, it takes a realization that change is needed; it needs new strategies and the commitment of management to stay the course. But it can be done. This is the rationale for strategic retention. This book is a blueprint for increasing the retention of the employees you want to keep through a number of targeted strategies. The Forward that follows is an overview to the chapters and authors that provide this blueprint.

—**Don Sanders**

PUBLISHER'S COMMENTS

When I began InSync Press in 1998, after nearly thirty years in the publishing industry, I had three goals. The first of these goals was to focus on just a few topical areas, health care and organizational management/leadership being the two I determined to begin with. The second goal was to provide perspectives that often went outside what you might find in the larger publishing houses. My third goal, and this was related to the second, was to publish authors who were practical in their approach, authors who would stress application over theory, a focus on "how and what" in addition to the "why."

Retain, Don't Retrain brings all three of those goals together. First, it is about one of the most serious issues faced by organizations today: How to keep the employees you want to keep. Second, it goes beyond the remedies usually found in other books, remedies that deal only with compensation or only with what a manager can do in a limited role to look at the entire organization and the entire individual. In this sense I really feel that this book is not only groundbreaking, but also the book that truly answers the question that managers are asking, namely, **How do I keep the employees I really want to keep?** Finally, the reader will find a number of very practical ideas here.

The first two chapters are by Dr. Don Sanders. I have published Don before with his *"Secrets from the Golf Course"* series (*Go for the Green, Leadership Secrets from the Golf Course*). His first article is titled **Eight Steps toward Building a Culture of Retention**. In this article Don convincingly demonstrates that retention is often an organization-wide issue and that, where it is, turnover will continue until organizational, divisional or departmental senior leadership proactively takes steps to change the culture. His eight steps provide a practical methodology for any organization seeking to improve retention through a focused, top down approach.

Don's second article begins a theme that is consistent throughout the remainder of the book. This theme is that, even if the organization does not take on retention as a strategic initiative, the individual manager has tremendous influence on the levels of retention within his or her group. How can a manager retain the employees that are critical to achieving the goals of the department or division? In this article (**Retention through Leadership**) Don suggests that people want to work for leaders who are Caring and Competent, who Coach and Communicate, and who reflect a set of values actions and beliefs we call Character.

Carol Hacker, who has published extensively in the areas of hiring and retaining good employees (*The Costs of Bad Hiring Decisions and How to Avoid Them* and *The High Cost of Low Morale*), and with whom I have worked for the last eight years, presents three short articles of extremely topical interest. The first of these deals with the initial step in either retention or turnover— the hiring process. Carol provides practical suggestions on how to hire the right people in order to prevent turnover. Her ideas on listening and asking the right kinds of questions will help any company avoid hiring those who would become part of the turnover statistic.

Carol's second chapter is also very topical. Many organizations are now hiring a significant number of employees from the generations that followed the "boomers"—Generation X and Generation Y. Are they different? Do you need alternative retention strategies? A definite "Yes" to both questions, says Carol in her chapter, **Hiring and Retaining Generation X and Y Employees**.

Carol's third chapter is also timely and practical. As noted above the theme of this book is that turnover occurs at the "point of contact", that is, at the interaction of supervisor and supervised. When correcting an employee, what can you do to prevent an employee from becoming defensive? What are the do's and don'ts? Carol provides a template in **Giving Critical Feedback without Causing Defensiveness**.

Dr. Lew Losoncy is in the enviable position of having an industry within which to refine and sharpen his approach to employee retention through the strategy of encouragement. By day Dr. Lew, as he is known, is a practicing counselor, speaker and trainer for a division of Bristol-Meyers, but he is also the author of several books on management strategy. His chapter is designed to go beyond comfortable solutions. In **The Soul Secret to Employee Retention**, Lew challenges managers and supervisors to leave the organizational comfort zone and to look at each individual as a complete human being with needs and wants that, if met, will keep that employee within the organization.

Do you want to hear about retention from the perspective of the front line supervisor? Ed Rose's **From Dictator to Facilitator: Retaining Employees Through the ACTOR Strategy** speaks to the problems faced by a one-time, "kick-butt/take names" supervisor to one who learns to become truly effective by working with people rather than through them. I have included Ed's developmental approach to becoming an ACTOR as an appendix.

The next chapter also shakes up the old "retention paradigm." In terms of retention, most of the focus has traditionally been on the manager and the organization. David Cox, a practicing psychologist, suggests that some of it simply has to do with the employee and the employee's perception of events. He argues that the manager who understands this perception and helps coach the employee out of this situation will likely not only save the employee but significantly increase his or her productivity. I think that you will find David's article, **Cutting through the C.R.A.P. — Helping You and Your Employees Stay Healthy, Happy and Productive**, a refreshing and innovative approach to one facet of the retention issue.

Nineteen eighty-four is known as the watershed year when the unwritten contract between employee and employer in the United States was forever changed. That was the year when layoffs, restructurings, and major mergers erased the employee-employer loyalty assumption. Prior to that date, it was assumed that, if you worked hard and were productive, you could have a job with your company forever. But, beginning in 1984, all that began to change.

In her two chapters, Teri Yanovitch argues that companies need to re-think this approach in terms of their most valued employees. Teri, who was a vice-president for Philip Crosby Associates and has spent the last 6 years in the business programs division of Walt Disney World, shows the importance of employee loyalty in maintaining customer loyalty (**The Loyalty Equation**) and the critical role of employee PRIDE in keeping the employees you want (**PRIDE Goeth before Retention**).

Where will the next generation of retention ideas come from? David Baker, Ph.D. founder of Renewal Associates, suggests that we will be looking for new solutions on the spiritual side. As a matter of fact, he advocates in his chapter, **Bottom-Line Spiritual** that it is on the spiritual side of each employee where the decision to stay or go is often made. David's contribution to retention strategies proposes that the seemingly most impractical approach (spiritual) may indeed be the most practical when seeking to keep your best employees. Spiritual is not religious, but goes beyond rules and beliefs about God to the essence of who we are. David says: serve this essence and keep your employees.

Finally, the question that everyone asks, "What about money? In the final chapter to the book, Don Sanders examines the role of compensation in retention and points out why some compensation plans actually encourage turnover. This final article, **Is that Your Final Question — The Role of Compensation in Employee Retention** explores the do's and don'ts of salaries and benefits in terms of employee retention.

I hope that you find these materials enlightening and helpful. It is mind-boggling to me that, according to the Thomas Staffings 14th Annual Survey Report, 65% of US companies do nothing to find out why employees leave and that almost half do nothing to reduce turnover. Turnover is an enormous cost to the company, the customer and the employee. We can do something about it. This book provides the why, the what and the how of strategic retention—the process of keeping the employees you want to keep.

—**Dennis McClellan**
Publisher

ABOUT
THE AUTHORS

DR. DON SANDERS

Senior author and editor of **Retain or Retrain**, Don's experience in management and leadership in both the public and private sector is reflected in his understanding of both the challenge and importance of the managerial role. Currently a speaker, author and consultant, the knowledge gained from working with over one hundred organizations, his own experience as a leader, and his extensive "hands on" research in employee retention, provide the underpinning for his practical approach to the problem. Don is also author of *Go For the Green—Leadership Secrets from the Golf Course* (InSync Press, 2001). Don received his Bachelors from UCLA and his Masters and Doctorate from the University of Oregon. He lives in Houston, Texas with his wife Angie within walking distance of Hole #1 of the "Old Course" at Raveneaux.

CAROL HACKER

Carol A. Hacker is president of Carol A. Hacker and Associates, a leading training and consulting company headquartered in Alpharetta, Georgia. For more that two decades Carol has been a significant voice in front line and corporate human resource management. Carol is also the author of numerous fine books including

The Costs of Bad Hiring Decisions & How to Avoid Them (CRC Press, 1999) and *The High Cost of Low Morale and What To Do About It* (St. Lucie Press, 1997). Carol received her B.S and M.S. with honors from the University of Wisconsin.

DR. LEW LOSONCY

Lew Losoncy has served for many years as psychologist for Matrix Essentials, formerly a division of Bristol-Myers Squibb and most recently a division of L'Oreal. Dr. Lew has been featured in news and print in publications as varied as *The Wall Street Journal*, *Psychology Today* and *Working Woman* and has been featured on *CBS This Morning* and *CNN*. He is the author of sixteen books including *The Motivating Team Leader*, *Turning People On*, and *What Is, Is* (with his wife Diane Losoncy). He lives in Wyomissing, Pennsylvania with Diane and their daughter Gabrielle Anna.

DAVID BAKER

David Baker, Ph.D. is the founder and Director of Renewal Associates, Inc., an educational and consulting agency that provides resources for those in the helping professions. He is a pastoral counselor in private practice in Orlando, Florida, where he is developing curriculum and experiences which focus on the integration of the psychological and the spiritual. He holds undergraduate and graduate degrees in theology and has a doctoral in clinical psychology. On weekends he plays drums with a jazz trio. He lives in Orlando with his wife Becky, sons Tristan and Dylan and Hobie the cat.

TERI YANOVITCH

Before founding her own company, Teri began her career working with leading international companies in training, consulting and customer service. She was regional trainer for the Hertz Corporation in the Southeastern United States and Caribbean. She later joined Philip Crosby and Associates and quickly rose to the position of Vice-President. She currently heads her own business, T.A. Yanovitch, Inc. and is a seminar speaker for Walt Disney world in their business programs division. She lives in Longwood, Florida with her husband and two children. She is a member of the National Speakers Association and is on the Board of Directors of Southern Ballet in Orlando.

ED ROSE

Currently Training Manager at Intersil Corporation in Palm Bay, Florida, Ed is a graduate of Warner Southern College with honors in Organizational Management. He is author of *Presenting and Training with Magic*, published by McGraw-Hill, *50 Ways To Teach Your Learner*, published by Jossey-Bass Pfeiffer, and *The Trainer's Role in The Successful Transition To Self- Directed Work Teams*, published by ASTD. Ed has 32 years experience in manufacturing, served as quality examiner for the State of Florida, and has published numerous papers on the subject of self-directed work teams. Frequent presenter at the ASTD and AQP National Conferences, the University of North Texas International Conference on Work Teams, and other national organizations Ed is a member of the International Brotherhood of Magicians and the International Magicians Society. Ed has played on 20 world championship softball teams and has been selected to eight all-world teams. He was inducted into the Senior Player's hall of fame in 1999.

DR. DAVID COX

A specialist in rehabilitation, neuropsychology and medical psychology throughout his career, David has held appointments at the

University of California at San Diego Medical Center, Duke University Medical Center and the University of North Carolina at Chapel Hill. He is currently Courtesy Professor of Clinical and Health Psychology at the University of Florida. Dr. Cox has served as a consultant to businesses in screening potential employees, evaluating current employees for advancement, facilitating employee exits and working on interactive processes to increase team efficiency and productivity. He worked with IBM to develop the THINKable program for individuals with brain injuries and other cognitive dysfunction. He is President of the Florida Psychological Association and serves on the Board of Directors of the American Cancer Society, Orlando Metro Unit, the American Academy of Doctors of Psychology and the Brain Injury Association of Florida.

BUILDING A CULTURE OF STRATEGIC RETENTION

The Eight Steps To Keeping the Employees You Want to Keep

by Donald Sanders, Ph.D.

OVERVIEW

This initial chapter provides a macro-approach to the issue of retention. It shows how a company or a department can implement a process of strategic retention by adopting a systematic and comprehensive eight-step approach. The implementation of these eight steps ensures that retention becomes not just another problem to deal with, but an integral part of the responsibility of each supervisor and manager.

INTRODUCTION

"I love working here. I have received two promotions in the past four years and I find my work really challenging. Jim (my manager) makes it a point to visit..."

I was at an off site location in the Southwest interviewing Joan and listening to her tell me why she wouldn't think of leaving EMCO[1] even though she wasn't located at corporate. It was the fall of 1996; I had been commissioned by EMCO to complete an employee survey because they were experiencing extremely high levels of turnover in some divisions (particularly the off-site or "remote" locations). The turnover in these divisions was running about forty percent above the industry norm. I interviewed more than fifty employees, some of which had left the company, others who were happy in their positions and a third group who were leaving as soon as conditions allowed. Embedded in the survey questions were several that were designed to elicit directly or indirectly the reasons that people were leaving the company.

The following are answers to the same question by two employees: one employee had been with the company for more than fifteen years and was planning on staying; the second employee had been with the company for six years and had just turned in her resignation. Their responses are so representative and so classic in terms of how to keep and how to lose good employees that they provide a blueprint for a strategy of building a "culture of retention" within any organization.

The first interview, the one that introduces this article, was with Joan. Joan was an experienced IT project manager who was working at a remote location. She was a single mother with two boys (ages 10 and 12) who enjoyed reading and running (not just after the boys, but real running as in marathons). Here is Joan's

---

[1] Names of companies and individuals have been changed to protect privacy.

answer to the question: "What is the best thing about working for EMCO?"

"I love working here. I have received two promotions in the past four years and I find my work really challenging. Jim (my manager) makes it a point to visit this site at least once a week and once or twice a month he takes us (Joan and other company employees at this site) to lunch and we talk about what is going on at the company and any problems we are having. He talks to my on-site manager here and makes sure that I stay in the loop. He understands what I am doing and he often discusses my projects with me both in person and over the phone. He is good at giving praise, although I must admit, I am my own harshest critic. You know, he sent me a company mouse pad with a picture of the six of us at lunch embedded in it. I really feel part of the company even though I am remote—and oh yes, they give me limited flex time. They know how important marathons are to me, so they will cut me some slack when I want to run my three or four marathons a year. My pay is competitive and the rest of the package, although not the best, is ok. Overall, they take care of me and it's a great company. I really wouldn't want to work anywhere else."

The second interview was with Roberta. Roberta was a help desk supervisor (there were five people working the help desk so she was also a "trouble shooter"). Like Joan, Roberta was working at a remote location. Also like Joan, she was a single mother. She had three children ranging in age from 6-11. She remarked that she didn't have time for any hobbies. Roberta's answer to the question: "What is the best thing about working for EMCO?"

"Nothing. The pay is average and the benefits second rate. I am always solving someone else's problem and I don't even know who it is that I work for. This is the third help desk job for me in four years with this company. I am ready for something new. I call my manager with a problem and he tells me that he will get back to me, but of course he doesn't. I haven't seen him in more than three months. I haven't had a formal review in eighteen months—what does that tell you? I am leaving as soon as I find something else. Do me a favor will you? Write in your report that employees who are ignored aren't motivated. If they are going to have remote sites, treat those employees like they belong to the company, not like unwanted step-children."

These two responses summarize what it is that you need to know to build a culture of retention. They succinctly represent the positions for "stay and leave." In literally thousands of interviews before and since, the same types of responses are given time and time again. We know what causes turnover; we know why some people stay while others leave, we know that some companies, some divisions and some departments do better at retaining key employees than others. The question is not the "what," it is the "how." Most companies simply don't know how to take what we know about retention strategy and make it an integral part of the organization. This article provides that "how;" it describes how to build a ***culture of strategic retention***[2] through the implementation of an eight step strategy:

1. **Commit to an Integrated and Systematic Retention Strategy**

2. **Make Retention a Part of the Manager's Job**

3. **Provide Defined Opportunities for Personal Growth**

4. **Involve Employees in an Enterprise Greater Than Themselves**

5. **Make Rewards Competitive**

6. **Demonstrate Respect for All Employees**

---

[2] There is no doubt that for some companies and in some industries retention of wanted employees (strategic retention) is more difficult than ever. With some "e-companies" offering immediate membership in the millionaires club, with the economy rushing along at 4-5% employment, and with the notion of company/employee and employee/company loyalty a vestige in many industries, retention of wanted employees is a challenge. But every organization can reduce turnover and increase retention by following these eight steps.

7. Add in a Dose of Fun

8. Build in "Differentiators"

STEP 1: COMMIT TO AN INTEGRATED, SYSTEMATIC RETENTION STRATEGY

Sitting in the rather spare offices of the Human Resources Manager at a major aerospace company in the late eighties, we came face to face with the company's retention problem. "Don, we have a major problem," he began. "We are losing a lot of good people. We begin by recruiting engineers at some of the best universities in the country (Duke, Notre Dame, Texas A&M, UCLA, Cal Tech). We bring them here at a good salary and within three years almost half are gone. By that time we have over a quarter of a million invested in each one what with salaries, learning curve time, and on site training. Within five years sixty percent are gone. I have taken a plan to the Division Vice-President, but he says that better recruiting and management training will solve the problem. What do you think?"

"I think recruiting and training will make a dent, but it won't solve the problem."

I had been down this road before so I was not surprised when I heard from the HR manager about two years later. "Well, like you said, we made a dent, but the problem is still enormous—and expensive. I have been offered a job in another state where I am promised top management support. So I am turning in my papers."

A paraphrase of the definition of insanity often attributed to Einstein applies here: "Insanity is doing the same things over and over and expecting a different result." Do you really want to improve the retention of wanted employees? Are you tired of losing from hundreds of thousands to millions of dollars in recruiting, hiring, training and learning curve costs? If you are, if you want to significantly and positively impact the turnover issues of the organization, you must make systemic changes to the organization that force this change to occur. Otherwise, you will continue to have the same results. Systemic changes may begin in Human Resources, but they require the visible and on-going support of the most senior leadership of the company. They require commitment.

Commitment means, "We will, in spite of what comes along." Commitment means that this focus on retaining key employees isn't a fad, flavor of the month or management by best seller. Commitment means that we are going to integrate this retention process into the values, mission and vision of the company whether these are written or not. Commitment means that the CEO or the president sees retention as a priority and is going to improve it—period.

Can you, as an individual manager or supervisor, impact turnover without senior level commitment? Certainly you can—at about seventy-five percent of the result you would get with commitment. Commitment is the fuel source—without it, there is little energy or power behind the initiative. If your senior management does not provide that fuel source, then each individual manager must.

But this chapter is about developing a company wide culture of retention, about getting 100% of the potential results, so, with senior management commitment, you are ready for Step 2—Making Retention a Part of the Manager's Job.

STEP 2: MAKE RETENTION A SYSTEMIC INITIATIVE AND A PART OF EVERY MANAGER'S JOB

We know how to reduce turnover on a company-wide level. It isn't a secret and hasn't been for some time. *The Service Profit Chain* by Heskett, Sasser and Schlesinger (1997: Free Press) demonstrates that there is a direct correlation between the full implementation of employee satisfaction strategies and employee loyalty (and company profitability!). We know beyond a doubt what to do to reduce turnover. The real question is: Knowing that the cost of turnover runs from the many thousands to the hundreds of millions dollars depending on the size of the company, why don't more companies do something about it? The answer is that most don't know what to do to systematize this process. Let's see how this can be done.

Consulting in the area of Leadership's role in Quality Improvement from 1988-1998, I was commissioned to complete a number of surveys or "needs assessments" on the perspective of employees on quality in general and continuous improvement in particular. What would you suppose was the most frequently heard response to the question: "How do you see Quality and Continuous Improvement in relation to what you do at this company?"

Do you suppose that people responded, "Quality is my job and the job of everyone at this company," or "I work every day to improve the things I do and the way my people serve their customers?" Well, they didn't.

In fact, what most people said was something along the lines of, "I do the best I can to do things right around here; the Quality Department takes care of quality and continuous improvement. Sure, I'll serve on a team, but quality is not my job."

It is now the year 2000 and some companies, Baldrige Award winners, Motorola, General Electric, Xerox, Hewlett-Packard and a host of others have so ingrained a quality as continuous improvement mentality into their culture that employees have simply accepted the fact that improvement is an ongoing expectation of working for one of these companies. It's part of the job.

And, as with quality in the eighties and through the mid nineties, the major issue in many companies today is retention.

Furthermore there are many companies who have problems of retention and don't even know they do. As it was with lack of quality, lack of retention (high turnover) is often a hidden cost of business. **And a final parallel between the quality problems of yesterday and the retention problems today is that few companies measure their cost and even fewer organize to attack the problem systematically.** So, to reduce turnover of unwanted employees, a sense of it's everyone's job must be integrated into the culture. How? Measure!

Once of the most enduring and accurate business dictums is: "What gets measured gets managed." Now certainly some organizations have trivialized this notion by trying to measure everything and thus managing nothing. But a balanced approach to measuring key processes and results helps any organization focus in on the goals it wants to achieve. So let's look at a balanced approach to measurement that will encourage managers to see retaining good employees as part of their job.

The idea of a balanced approach to measurement is not new, it has just lost currency with our recent emphasis on financial data. In 1990, the Nolan Norton institute, a research arm of KPMG, sponsored a multi-company study *"Measuring Performance in the Organization of the Future."* The hunch behind the study was that over-reliance on financial performance data were impeding the ability of an organization to "create future economic value."

Out of this study came an article in the Harvard Business Review (January-February, 1992) titled, *"The Balanced Scorecard— Measures that Drive Performance"* by Robert Kaplan and David Norton. In 1996 the Harvard Business School Press published a book by the same title *The Balanced Scorecard* which was to become a business best-seller.

Why do you need to know this? Because Kaplan and Norton offer documented case studies of the positive impact of a balanced scorecard approach (financials are simply lagging indicators of how well you have done in other areas—they represent the result of other efforts) and because "Learning and Growth" and "Internal Business Processes" are two of the four perspectives of the Balanced Scorecard. And this is where you make retention a systemic part of the company through company wide initiatives, measurement and alignment. Make retention a line in the supervisor's and manager's job description, hold every manager responsible, meet with managers on a monthly or quarterly basis to review potential problems related to retention of good employees. Build retention responsibility into the system.

If you don't make this initiative systemic, if some departments or divisions buy in while others don't, if you just make retention a part of some parts of the company, but not others, of some managers, but not others, you will achieve more than if you did nothing. But not making the initiative systemic, not building it into processes, procedures, job descriptions, performance reviews, compensation strategies and the like, for all managers, leaves you open to the following types of problems, illustrated by an incident that was related to me by the first mate of a small freighter after his resignation.

"Look, they told me I was responsible for retention, that part of my job was to make sure that the crew stayed with the ship for the entire trip. But we lost three guys at the first port and two more at the second. The Captain jumped all over me. I told him that I would never have hired those guys in the first place; that they weren't cut out for this type of work, for this type of environment. The Captain said that that was my problem, and I should have been more creative in dealing with those guys; he said every first mate in the fleet had similar problems and they weren't running twenty percent turnover in two weeks. So, I quit. With my skills, I can get a job anywhere I want."

What happened here? Why did this company lose both a good manager and some critical crew members? The reason was stated clearly by this man. The company had not made retention a systemic expectation of every manager. As this employee noted later, "They gave me all kinds of responsibility and accountability with no authority. I know that seasoned hands are hard to find, but those guys should never have been offered a job. They were turnover waiting to happen."

So, a warning about making retention a part of every manager's job; **you cannot give retention accountability without some retention responsibility**. If I, as a manager or supervisor, have to take the people that HR sends me, or the trouble maker that no one else wants, or the individual who has worked for seven employers during the last three years, I am likely being set up for failure. If, as an organization, you are going to take the most effective step toward building a culture of retention, that is, making retention an integral performance expectation for all managers, then make sure that the managers have authority as well as responsibility for keeping valued employees.

As Carol Hacker notes in her book, *The Cost of Bad Hiring Decisions and How to Avoid Them*, high retention rates of the people you want to keep begin with recruiting and hiring the right people. Involve managers from the beginning of the process. Make sure that the "specifications" (experience, education, skills) are reviewed and approved by the manager before the recruitment and hiring process begins. Then let the manager be part of the review and selection process and ensure that this manager is involved in compensation decisions for the individual wherever possible. You will not only lose fewer employees, you will lose fewer "first mates."

So, you have made the commitment to a retention strategy and systematically integrated the responsibility for retention into the job descriptions of all managers. The next step is to give those managers the tools to effectively implement this requirement. In other words, the managers might say, "Okay, you want me to reduce turnover and keep the people we want to keep, how am I supposed to do this?" The next four steps answer this question.

STEP 3: PROVIDE DEFINED PERSONAL GROWTH OPPORTUNITIES FOR ALL EMPLOYEES

Managers often have one of two unstated (and often unconscious) beliefs. The first of these is, "If I train someone to take my position, I am expendable." The second is, "If I train someone to take my position, I am promotable." The first position is a "glass is half-empty" or pessimistic viewpoint that, in its narrowness of vision, sends a message to employees that "This department or division is doing just fine as it is and will remain static as long as I am in charge." Few employees want to work in this environment.

The second position is a "glass is half full" or optimistic management perspective. It says to the employee, "We are dynamic and entrepreneurial, we are dedicated to growth. If you want to be part of this team, get ready for personal growth."

This is the environment that the majority of today's workers want to work in. In literally hundreds of workshops with literally thousands of employees and managers, I have asked participants to list their top five motivators and their top five "de-motivators." Unfailingly, one of the top five motivators is "Challenge and opportunity for personal growth." On the flip side, a consistent de-motivator is "Nowhere to go, stuck in a position."

People thrive on hope, they want to see things improve; most want to improve themselves, to learn new things. Perhaps your company cannot promote all those who want to be promoted; not every customer service representative can become a customer service manager. But you can provide growth opportunities such as customer service training, team building, phone etiquette and skills, basic sales and communication techniques. The list is endless. When you train people, when you provide growth opportunities, you not only benefit the employee, you benefit the company.

"Yeah, but if I train them, they leave." This is a direct quote from a manager at a mid-sized company with no formal training program when I suggested that part of her turnover problem was failure to train, failure to provide opportunities for growth.

And my reply was, "Yes, some will. But most won't. Not if you see retention as a systemic issue. If you just train, then some will leave, but if you train people, and if you establish parallel compensation systems that reward not just managers, but highly competent workers, and if you integrate respect and recognition with a little fun on the job, the great majority won't leave. The key is to see it as a comprehensive retention system, rather than separate and distinct parts of a retention effort."

STEP 4: INVOLVE THEM IN AN ENTERPRISE GREATER THAN THEMSELVES

There is a story that is frequently told in training circles that is attributed to Charles Schwab. It is the story is of three workers who were laying brick. The first one is asked, "What are you doing?" He responds, "I am laying brick." The second is also asked, "What are you doing," and he responds by saying, "I am making fifteen dollars and hour." Finally, the third one is asked, "What are you doing?" He responds with, "I am helping to build a great cathedral."

My belief is that most workers want to be involved, not in laying brick or just making money, but in building great cathedrals. Most people want to leave legacies, they want their time and their life to mean something. They want to be able to look back and say I created that.

Twenty years ago, when Silicone Valley was still greater San Jose, when VC still referred to Viet Cong, not Venture Capital, when monitors had this fuzzy green tint and IBM bet the bank on main frames, some few entrepreneurs created a technological revolution, which is today driving our productivity and economy.

These entrepreneurs gave their people that sense of building great cathedrals. The enthusiasm and commitment that was generated literally changed the world. People knew it was a race, they knew that the opportunities were immense and the challenges were limitless. The stories of the early days of Silicon Valley leave no doubt but that employees realized they were involved in something greater than themselves.

"What about me?" you respond. I don't have a start up, I am managing a group of engineers, accountants, schedulers, sales people etc. in a mature industry. Where is my cathedral?"

The answer is that everyone has a cathedral called excellence. Your goal as a manager/leader should be to inspire everyone to make your company, your division, your region, your department, your branch, your group, the best in the company. Do it in a "rah, rah fashion" if you are a "rah, rah leader", in a subdued fashion if you are a quiet and analytical leader. But do it. If you are a manager, let everyone know that he or she is part of the team and that your goal pure and simple is to be known as the best team in the entire organization. If you are an owner or CEO, let everyone in the company know that mediocrity is not acceptable, that your goal is to be the best in the industry. Let Excellence be your flag

When you do this, no matter how you do it, people feel part of a process greater than themselves—and keep raising the bar. Praise and raise, praise and raise, until all people are performing at their best level. You will find more people wanting to join this team than to leave it. People actively pursue excellence and are de-motivated by sustained and seemingly inescapable mediocrity.

STEP 5: MAKE REWARDS COMPETITIVE WITH THE INDUSTRY

About five years ago I was making a presentation to more than six hundred owners and managers of a major oil company's distribution centers ("service stations"). At the end of my presentation, which was all about the importance of the personal touch and quality service, we had a question and answer session.

Right out of the box a hand went up in the front row. "Have you ever run a gas station?" (Notice the term—"gas" not "service").

"No," I replied.

"Well, then, let me tell you how it really is. They will drive across the street for a penny a gallon savings. There is no loyalty in our business. It's a commodity."

Like this service station owner, many managers believe that their people will leave them for a dollar an hour raise, for a five thousand dollar a year raise, for a pay raise that is not too terribly more than what they are getting today. But like the service station owner who doesn't want to look at what he is not doing, thus being able to blame all defections on price, many managers don't want to look at what they are not doing with their people thus blaming all defections on money issues.

My response to this service station owner is the same one I give to managers. I said, "I understand that customers will drive across the street for a penny a gallon if you don't do the things I was talking about, but if you give them friendly, personalized service, if you do the little things that add up like maintaining a clean and shining appearance everywhere in the station, if you thank them seriously for their business and don't treat them like a commodity, if you carry the products that they need, they won't leave you for a penny, probably not even for a nickel a gallon, but they will leave you for eight and almost assuredly for ten cents a gallon."

Compensation is an issue, no doubt about it; and fair compensation is a topic to itself. What we know is that today's worker looks at compensation as a measure of the value the organization places on that individual as a contributor to the organization. If your salaries are far below the average salary paid for doing the same work—and if there are options open—people will leave because of money. The secret to fair compensation is to pay at least the average salary for that kind of work in that industry in that area—and then to look at what else you can do to augment this through appropriate profit sharing, pension, 401k and other financial benefits that are available to you. (For more details on how to build a compensation strategy that increases retention, see my chapter titled: **Compensation and Retention**).

Look at the cost of turnover and you may find that involving everyone, not just the executive group or the management group, in profit sharing is an opportunity for significant return on investment.

STEP 6: DEMONSTRATE RESPECT FOR ALL EMPLOYEES

"I told my employees, if they will just row, I will steer the boat." It was one of those moments when a basic belief system was explained in such a jarring metaphor that it was forever imprinted in my mind.

We were returning from dinner after a day-long presentation on motivation, change and turnover when this manager said this to the five of us in the van. To be honest, we all smiled because of the source. This manager, an extremely bright and dedicated "driving driver" type who was having turnover and performance problems (even while he delivered "results"), didn't realize that the days of being admiral of the fleet while his employees toiled below decks, went out with the Roman Trireme.

A week later, I was with some of this manager's employees along with several hundred others at a similar presentation. When we got to de-motivators, the issue of respect came up.

"He doesn't respect us, and it is a major de-motivator," said one manager.

"What do you mean, not respect you", I asked. "Tell me what that means."

"It means that he won't listen to our ideas, he talks, but he doesn't listen, he acts as if he is the only one who knows anything about this business."

Another chimed in, "I have been working in the warehouse for two years now. Before that I was in another warehouse in the company. I can see ten things we could do tomorrow to improve things and make more money. I tried to talk to him about these ideas and he told me to just make sure the work got done. That was my job."

This is the operational definition of "lack of respect" in the eyes of the worker. As a manager, you obviously cannot take most of the suggestions given to you by those you supervise, they often don't understand the external context. But you can implement some of those ideas and certainly you can respectfully listen and respond when ideas are shared with you.

Simply taking time, simply acknowledging that this individual is worthy of your attention is a way of showing respect. Again, a little time pays big dividends.

I need to quickly mention two other respect issues. Please do not manage by e-mail or memo. People consider it a sign of respect when you talk to them personally. It may be more efficient to use memos or e-mail, but it certainly is not as effective. Use e-mails only where it really makes sense to do so, not to manage your department.

Finally, walk your talk and show respect to people when you meet with them regularly to discuss goals and progress; get to know them as people. Let your people know that what they are doing is important, that they are helping to achieve the goals of the organization. Share whatever information you can. Giving of your time is a precious gift for most employees.

STEP 7: ADD IN A DOSE OF FUN

Janice was an IT manager at a transportation company. Naturally outgoing and creative, she was faced with significant turnover when she decided to do something about it. She decided to add a dose of fun. She sent the daily joke of the day (always tasteful) via e-mail. She held contests over lunch, she took the group bowling, she did a "ropes" day and the highlight of the year, she held a "Gong Show" where, among other talented (and not so talented) presentations, she was spoofed by some of her employees. She let them be creative in presenting innovations to the company and even sponsored her own "hospitality room" at all company meeting. Turnover plummeted, loyalty increased. In an area where job hopping was commonplace, she created a stable organization.

"Whoa", you say. "I can show respect, I can listen, I can even create an atmosphere where people feel that they are involved in something greater than themselves. But fun? I am not that kind of person."

So delegate. Do what one client did when they appointed a "Director of Fun." If you aren't the creative, innovative fun type, then find someone who is and turn it over to them. But do it! Having fun together creates a sense of camaraderie and teamwork that is almost impossible to create any other way. Group enjoyment increases loyalty and reduces turnover.

STEP 8: BUILD IN "DIFFERENTIATORS"

It really does not matter whether we are in an economy as strong as the one we are currently in or a slower one with a higher rate of the "unemployed" available to choose from: if you want to hire and keep the best you must differentiate yourself from the competition.

In sales, this is called having a USP, a Unique Selling Position. In retention it is called having "differentiators." What are differentiators? They are the small, but important benefits that make your company stand out in the minds of your employees. Differentiators show you care, they are commonplace in the companies that qualify as part of Fortune's 100 Best companies to work for.

For example, Lucent Technologies provides up to $7,000 per year toward undergraduate study, Four Seasons comps hotel stays for their employees, American Century provides ergonomic chairs and wellness benefits, Amgen provides on-site child care. Genetech makes available a six-week annual sabbatical and unlimited paid sick days, David Weekly homes flew its 543 "Team Members" (staff) to Maui in 1999 and expects to fly them to the Caymans in 2000. Pfizer gave 150 shares of stock to each employee in 1999 (and of course, prescriptions are free). Many top companies pick up 100% of health premiums and CISCO provides up to $2,000 on the spot for outstanding contributions.

Differentiators range from stock options to massages, from child care to liberal leave, from donuts and bagels with the CEO to all expense paid trips to Pebble Beach. More than anything, they are an indicator that the company truly cares about the well being of its employees. So, be creative, challenge and change the culture of your company and the industry, build in differentiators.

SUMMARY

Every organization, every company, every region, division, and department can do things to increase the retention of valued employees. The most important steps you can take include making a commitment to reduce unwanted turnover, integrating retention expectations into every managers' job, providing opportunities for personal growth, involving people in something greater than themselves, reviewing your reward system and ensuring that it is competitive while demonstrating respect for all employees and adding in a dose of fun and a differentiator or two.

If you take these steps, you will significantly reduce the loss of valued employees.

The next chapter provides strategies for the individual manager to use. What do you think is the one single thing that a manager can use to reduce turnover within his or her department. Did you guess "increase their salary?" If you did...

RETENTION THROUGH LEADERSHIP

*The Five "C's" in Becoming the Leader
People Want to Work for*

by Donald Sanders, Ph.D.

OVERVIEW

Why is it that some supervisors have a lot of turnover and others very little? Why is it that even in some high demand professions some companies and some departments have high turnover while others have little or none? Some of it goes back to what we discussed in the first chapter, differentiators, involvement in something special and fun. But much of it comes down to the individual manager or leader. How that individual leads his or her employees is usually the single most critical factor in strategic retention. If we can move managers to become leaders using the "Five C's" we can dramatically reduce unwanted turnover.

INTRODUCTION

Did you guess, "Pay them more money," or "Increase their compensation" at the end of the last chapter? If you did, you may not know a "Jim." Jim had a different solution.

It was a training class being presented to thirty managers, primarily from the engineering and marketing departments and the usual banter was taking place before the training started.

One manager asked another, "Hey Jim, is Terry still leaving?"

Jim was visibly embarrassed. "No," he replied. "Well, why not," chided the other manager, "I hear the competition offered him a significant increase in pay to jump ship."

"Yes, yes they did," he replied.

"So, why isn't he leaving?"

"Well... he said it was because he really liked working for me."

A good deal of kidding followed that remark, but the division manager came up to me at the break. "That was real," he said. "Jim has lost fewer than three people in his department of twenty-seven over the last five years when our company average is about 20-25%. He doesn't pay any better than anyone else, but his retention rate of good people is excellent. Why? What we want from this class is more 'Jim's'."

In the previous chapter I discussed how to build a culture of strategic retention, how to integrate retention strategies into the fabric of the company. But even the best retention culture will falter on the negative behavior of the people who must implement it, particularly in terms of leadership characteristics. The following five characteristics continuously recur as themes in the literature on leadership. Some are not new, but few are practiced on a regular basis by all managers, and, as a result, people often leave organizations with the spoken or unspoken reason, "I just couldn't work with (or for) my manager. Interestingly, the five essential characteristics of a retention-based leader all begin with "C;" they are:

CHARACTER

CARING

COMMUNICATION

COACHING

COMPETENCE

Before we examine each of these, it is important that we define the role of the leader. What is the leader's job? What can the leader do to help build a culture of retention? In John Kotter's most recent book, *John P. Kotter on What Leaders Really Do* (Harvard Business School Press, 1999), the author states unequivocally that, "Institutionalizing a leadership centered culture is the ultimate act of leadership." In other words, the job of the leader is to establish a culture where everyone has leadership opportunities, growth opportunities, and challenge. What Kotter does not say, but what follows directly from this philosophy is that if you do so, you will reduce unwanted turnover and increase retention of the employees you want to keep.

Leadership is a discipline, it has an underlying structure built on a knowledge of what works. It is not a vague sense of control or, as many have said to me, "I have been a manager for ten years and I can make this work," or "I know what's best for everyone." Rather, leadership is a discipline built on years of research, years of observing and chronicaling what works and what doesn't. Much of it is summarized in the Five "C's." So, let's examine how you can "C" your way to retention through leadership.

STEP 1: DEMONSTRATING LEADERSHIP CHARACTER

The first and absolutely most critical aspect of leadership is character. It has been well noted that "Who you are speaks greater volumes than what you say." People gravitate towards the leadership character that includes integrity, authenticity, fairness, the ability to inspire and personal courage. Let's look at each one of these individually.

INTEGRITY is consistency between what you believe, what you say and what you do. Integrity includes both honesty and authenticity. Honesty is highly valued and all too rarely displayed, usually with the rationalization, "If I told them the truth, they couldn't handle it." In fact the reality might be that if you told them the truth about the seriousness of a problem or a financial uncertainty, they might rally—it often depends on the other leadership qualities you bring to the table. Remember, managers rigidly control information and leaders judiciously share information.

Of course there are times when the demands of public responsibility, stockholder value or just plain common sense will tell you that this is not the time to be totally forthright, but these times are rare. More often we find a failure of leadership when people in leadership positions don't want to face the consequences of telling the truth. Two potentially great presidents (Nixon and Clinton) lost the opportunity of having supporters rally around them when they lied to the public. People will respect you if you can say, "I made a mistake and am resolved not to do it again"—as long as it only happens once or twice. But failure to be honest destroys perceived leadership character; it destroys the willingness of people to follow you. Without integrity there is no trust and without trust there is no leadership.

AUTHENTICITY is equally important in a leader. Authenticity is being who you are without pretense, without apology and without phoniness. The problem is that in our culture many of us are shaped by media and particularly by the images of the "successful." These images of success rarely leave our conscious and unconscious awareness as they are hammered at us through television, movies, and magazines. We have images for success as a rock star, as a movie star, as an executive, as a salesperson, as an athlete—the images are endless, and often erroneous. It is easier to adopt a stereotypical image than it is to be authentically who we are.

If you question whether you are perceived as an authentic leader, go back to your beliefs. Clarify these beliefs, write them down (it is hard to be authentic to beliefs that are either unformed or unconscious) . What are your beliefs about the people you lead? Do you believe that people are basically good and eager to work or lazy and in need of constant supervision? Do you believe that most people seek challenge, or do you believe that most people just want to put in their hours and go home to their TV? In their perceptive book on coaching, *Everyone's a Coach* (Harper Business Books, 1995) Don Shula and Ken Blanchard note that becoming an effective coach begins with being conviction driven, that is, by knowing what you stand for and living your life in concert with those beliefs. It is the same for leaders. Determine your beliefs, determine what you stand for and then be authentic, live according to those beliefs.

Obviously the problem is that too few of us ever take time to examine our beliefs; as a result, we often miss the most basic reason that we have not attained our leadership goals. So, let's see what your basic leadership beliefs are. Take a few minutes to think this through; if you cannot do it now, complete it later (See Table on the following page). Beliefs are the foundation of being an authentic leader.

**MY FIVE BASIC BELIEFS ABOUT
MANAGING AND LEADING OTHERS:**

1. _____

2. _____

3. _____

4. _____

5. _____

There are few complaints heard more about managers than that the individual is not "fair." **FAIRNESS** is one of the most challenging aspects of being a leader. Because fairness is often in the eye of the beholder and because many people consider only how a given action impacts them, it is nearly impossible to be fair in the eyes of all the people you manage. The best that you can typically do here is to treat everyone with respect and to share personal rationales for some of your decisions. Obviously, it is important to treat everyone equally particularly with respect to "rules."

Support for this is found in one of my favorite quotes from Don Shula, former coach of the Miami Dolphins and winningest coach in NFL history. Shula says,

"You can't let poor performance go unnoticed—even from a superstar."

Yet many managers do. They have one set of standards for a high performer and another set for everyone else. As a speaker and consultant I have heard of horror stories from attendees and witnessed the decline of morale when favoritism was shown. In one company there was a hard and fast rule that everyone was to be ready to talk to a customer by 8:00 AM. Everyone except Denise, of course. Denise was part of the team but didn't want to play by the rules. She would regularly arrive at work at 8:20, 8:30 or later. Denise was bright, brash and intimidating. Excellent with customers, she was a top producer when she was there, and she reported that she usually stayed until 6 or 6:30 (although management was not typically there to verify this) when others left at 5:00. Her supervisor failed to confront her—in no part because she was both intimidating and able to walk into the office of a senior vice-president and present her case.

The result was more than just the continued grumbling within the department. Others started coming in later and later; after all, if Denise could break the rule, why couldn't they? Suddenly, there was only one person to answer the phone, not six or seven, at eight in the morning. Suddenly, there were long lunches and too many personal phone calls. Suddenly, there was a major morale problem; suddenly, sales began falling off. Finally, after losing two good employees and seeing sales decline, the manager called a team meeting—at 8:00 in the morning. Denise wasn't there (running late of course—a brilliant strategy by the manager). The other team members expressed their frustration at having two sets of rules; they said that it wasn't fair that Denise got to live by one set of rules while the rest of them were held to another set. The supervisor listened carefully, took notes, said he understood and promised that the problem would be taken care of.

I wish I could tell you that this story had a happy ending, one that readers would want to emulate, but it didn't. If you have had any experience in corporate America, you may have already guessed what happened. Denise was transferred. No corrective moment, no re-direction, no explanation that this behavior was unacceptable. It was a classic lose/lose/lose/lose managerial moment. The team lost good employees and their perception of the supervisor as being fair. The supervisor lost credibility and an opportunity to test himself. Denise lost an opportunity to grow and to become a part of the team—as talented as she was she never got promoted. She was aware of the fact that she had intimidated this supervisor and quietly let others know "she won." And finally, the company lost—sales, employees, customers and the potential of a gifted team member. Being perceived as fair is critical for leaders. "Never let poor performance go unnoticed—even from a superstar."

A third facet of the leadership character is the ability to **INSPIRE**. This does not mean that you have to be an outgoing, rah-rah leader. Inspire means to breathe life into something. Leaders do this, some quietly, some effusively, some dramatically, some analytically, but leaders that others want to work for and follow, inspire others to want to achieve something special, to feel a part of a team, to perform to the best of their abilities—this is the type of inspiration that people look for.

Few things inspire more than a vision. An overworked word, vision, but one that makes such a difference when it is established and implemented. Three related words are inspire, vision and enthusiasm. When you create a vision for your department, division, region or company, you inspire your people. The result is enthusiasm. As we all know, enthusiasm is contagious.

"Whoa! Stop right there." Many managers say, "That's not me, I have integrity, I can be fair, and I am as authentic as they come, but I do my job quietly. I don't do vision and I am not charismatic."

There are two responses to this common objection: first, you don't need to be charismatic to inspire people, you just need to paint a picture of where the organization is going and how it is going to get there; second, being a leader is not "natural" for most of us—you must step out of the comfort zone if you truly wish to lead others, you must sometimes do what is difficult. This leads us to the final leadership characteristic that we will discuss under the heading of character—courage.

COURAGE is taking action in the face of fear. It isn't absence of fear, it is taking action when you are aware of fear. I personally believe that fear, particularly fear of rejection and fear of interpersonal discomfort, has doomed more leadership careers than any other single factor. Volumes have been written on fear and why people get stuck in comfort zones; additional volumes have been written on how to overcome fear. They all boil down to this: "I can, because I do." In other words, to change your belief about the perception (not the fact) that you can't, do the thing that you think you cannot do.

There is a wonderful story of Bill Pinkey, the third American and first African-American to solo circumnavigate the globe. High school graduate and self-taught mariner, he was asked upon the successful conclusion of his voyage how he got the courage to face those thirty foot waves, high seas and other life threatening situations. His succinct reply tells us much about the courage needed to manage others. He said, "Those challenges didn't so much take courage as knowledge, determination and skill; courage was deciding to leave the dock."

In order to be an effective leader, you have to make your mind up that you are "going to leave the dock." This means that you will use your knowledge, determination and skill to confront that employee who is coming in late, even if it makes you terribly uncomfortable. You will make that speech to the team, you will practice in front of a mirror until it is your speech, then make that speech. You will sell them your vision. You will make that call that you don't want to make, talk to that supervisor who is costing you good people. Friedrich Nietzsche is quoted as saying, "Anything that does not kill us, makes us stronger." You will note that every time you take action in face of your fear, you become stronger. Of course you can inspire, you simply have to take action in face of your fear, you have to decide to leave the dock. And when you do, you will find that people decide that your organization is a great place to work.

STEP 2: CARING AS A CRITICAL CHARACTERISTIC OF LEADERS

Some managers, for some seemingly good reasons, don't want to have to "care" for employees. Their perspective is this:

"I am here to manage a department, to produce results, to achieve objectives and add to the bottom line. I am not here to baby-sit. If you want to work for me, I expect you to produce results like a professional. I don't have time to molly-coddle seventeen direct reports."

On the surface, you cannot argue with this perspective. Business is business and people are expected to be professional. But simple answers that reflect a simpler time are not the answer to the retention problem. The above quote is a classic "old style management perspective." It assumes that the role of the supervisor is to plan, direct, organize and control to produce results. But people are not easy to direct and control today. Today's employee is looking for leadership and leadership is about influence and skills not just control. Part of influencing others is showing that you have a genuine concern for both problems and people.

Ken Blanchard put this succinctly when he noted that "too many organizations seem to be organized as if the sheep were there for the benefit of the shepherd." What this means in practice is that people see all rewards flowing upward, and that many managers see their people as instruments for the manager's success. While these managers (and organizations) may have short-term success, long term they lose their most critical resource—the relationship between the employees of the company and the customers of the company. It reflects an attitude that says, "I will take, but not give, I will command, but not care."

In the stable environments of the past, even into the early eighties, this attitude worked, it made sense. In an era of rapid change, it does not. Managers focus on maintaining the system, leaders focus on changing it. As John Kotter notes, management is "hard and cool; leadership is "soft and hot." To prevent turnover, you need "soft and hot" skills, you need caring.

The Fallacy of the "Five P's"

Most managers and supervisors look at their jobs in terms of what I call the "Five P's." In other words, they see their job as a juggling act with projects, processes, paperwork, products and people all in the air at the same time. Their job is to make sure that none gets dropped. The truth of the matter is that managers and supervisors would have to worry less about the other four if they focused on the most important one—people. Not people as means to achieve tasks and produce results, but as integrally valuable human beings. A bit far out?

In James Kouzes and Barry Posner's most recent book, *Encouraging the Heart* (Jossey-Bass, 1999), they cite some startling results of research conducted by the Center for Creative Leadership. This nonprofit educational institution looked at critical variables for success in terms of the top three jobs in any organization. The number one factor? Relationships with subordinates.

Even more striking, however, was the research result on variables that differentiated the top and bottom quartile of managers. The one factor that consistently differentiated top performing managers from the also-rans was the ability to show warmth and fondness toward others. These high performing managers liked people and showed it. Kouzes noted that the best leaders give trust, respect and encouragement. They don't try to control, they liberate; they don't hold their cards up to their faces, they share rationales; they don't ignore feelings in the workplace, they acknowledge them.

A question that I am frequently asked by managers who are
working on their leadership skills is this; "If I have to choose
between being liked and being respected, which should I choose?"
My answer is "both." There is a reason that Blanchard and Shula
wrote *Coaching from the Heart*, and that Kouzes and Posner wrote
Encouraging the Heart. Today we know that you don't have to
trade off results for being liked, in fact you should have both.[1]
Combining a sense of caring for people with a sense of mission
about the purpose of the organization, is a dynamic tool to produce
superior results while maintaining the enthusiasm and loyalty of
your people. Caring leaders create loyal employees resulting in less
unwanted turnover.

STEP 3: BECOME A COMMUNICATOR

Too many managers look at their jobs not unlike that of a poker
player. As the poker player carefully draws his cards, retaining
some and discarding others, he holds them close to his chest,
ensuring that no other individual can see the cards he is holding or
know the strategy he is planning.

Once again, this strategy worked well thirty years ago, when
the job of most people in leadership roles was actually to manage.
It worked with a less educated workforce whose work ethic said, "I
am here to do a job; tell me what to do and I will get it done."

---

[1] For some this is not adequate. "But if you were really pressed, which one would you
choose?" they ask. Of course the answer is respect. Leaders are always respected (not
feared) even if they are not particularly well liked. But, if you truly care, if you accept only
the best from each employee because it is in the best interest of the employee, you will be
respected and liked.

But "the times they are a changin." The face of the workplace is changing dramatically. The demographics of yesterday are not the demographics of today, a younger, more independent, often better educated (in terms of formal education) population fills our companies and other organizations today. These people have different expectations. (See Carol Hacker's Chapter: **Recruiting and Retaining "Generation Y and X" Employees**).

A survey conducted by Public Allies, a Washington, DC based nonprofit, focused in on such a group. Their national survey, conducted only with 18-30 year olds, asked what they saw as the most critical aspects of leadership. The most frequent response was, "the ability to see a situation from another's point of view." (This was followed by being able to get along with others and then integrity.)

"Being able to see a situation from another's point of view." In other words, these workers wanted the leader to practice the skill of empathy, a critical communication skill.

Should we be surprised that there is a direct correlation between communication and leadership and another between leadership and retention? No. We have known for some time that communication is critical to leadership. As a matter of fact, most surveys suggest that somewhere between 75 and 90 percent of the job of leading people involves communication, so not working at improving this skill is self-defeating, something like trying to grow plants without water. Putting it more directly, lack of communication skills undermines the vision, the alignment, the goals, and the overall effectiveness of a leader. If you are not currently as effective as you would like to be in terms of communication, don't despair; communication skills can be learned, honed, and improved upon. In a phrase, "Managers talk, Leaders communicate." So, lets begin by visiting two extremes of communication to see why communicating, not just talking is so important.

A vice president of a major division within a large chemical company once said to me about his employees, "They are all like me—and if they aren't, they should be." He had called me in because a 360° assessment of his leadership style had indicated that people thought he was a poor communicator and because, relative to other divisions, his was suffering more than double the turnover in highly talented, relatively young professionals. We were sitting in his office having a discussion about his leadership style. I explained to Mike that one of the results of the survey I had recently completed was that his people thought he was not an effective communicator.

He sat forward in his chair, hands gripping the edge of the desk. "What do they mean I am not an effective communicator," he exploded. "I am out there in the halls and in the plant all the time. I am constantly telling people what is going on, I tell them what to do and how to do it. I tell them about directives from corporate and I tell them about how we are doing in terms of our measurements. If they don't hear me out there, I bring them in here and tell 'em again. If they don't hear me in this office, I suggest they look elsewhere. My division will perform!"

"Mike," I said, "I know that you really don't understand why this survey was necessary and I am sure you are frustrated at having to spend this time with me right now when there are other problems that need your immediate attention. I want to clearly say to you that it isn't the *telling* side of communication people are concerned about, you do that very well. It is the listening side of the communication equation that is the issue."

It was as if this thought had never crossed his mind. He honestly believed that his job was to talk, not hear, to tell rather than to listen. He was literally dumbfounded that he was not seen as a great communicator. His presentations were first rate, his written and verbal messages clear. Yet the chemical engineers and chemists that he was churning through represented an investment of about

$115,000 each (recruiting costs, relocation costs, mentoring costs, salaries) over two years at the time of this engagement—and they were losing this investment all too regularly. There was a significant gap in experience levels in his staff. There were long-termers who had found a way to work within his style (and who were building up their retirement benefits), and there were these bright, energetic youngsters with less than two years of experience who were still optimistic that the situation would improve—somehow. There were few employees with between two and nine years of experience. There was no up and coming leadership; those with leadership potential had decided to go elsewhere, to companies, departments and divisions who didn't equate leadership with position power and the sending, as opposed to, receiving, of messages.

About two years after Mike, I was working with a regional vice president who was having trouble meeting corporate goals in terms of both recruiting and placements. Gloria's problem was just the opposite of Mike's. She was a great listener, would empathize with the problems faced by staff in sales and recruiting, would work with people to come up with ideas; but she wouldn't hold their feet to the fire, she wouldn't demand results. She wouldn't tell, only ask.

In fact Gloria was as stuck in a management and communication paradigm as ineffective as Mike's. Her method was not leadership but rather an abdication of leadership. Like Mike, she was standing behind the troops rather than leading from the front.

Seeking an appropriate model for leadership, most of us are captured by the "tyranny of the or" when we should be examining the "freedom of the and."

This applies directly to management communication. Some managers seek to be leaders by always telling, others by never telling. Neither is effective. It is true that surveys have shown that effective leaders ask and listen more than they tell and order, but this does not point to an extreme, but to a balance. If your strength is in telling, commit to listen more, if it is in asking, commit to making firm requests and following up to ensure that the request is followed. Build on your strengths to minimize your weaknesses.

One more important word on communication. I sometimes have managers say to me, "I am working here with competent professionals, my job is budgeting and planning, these folks don't need anything from me." This is what I call an effort at "leadership by hope." Not only does it not work, it has a negative impact on morale. Ignoring people causes them to leave, mentally at first, then physically. When primitive tribes want to punish someone, they often ostracize that individual for a period of time or indefinitely. No one wants to work in a silent environment, the job of the leader is to develop others so that they can produce the required results, you cannot do this in a silent environment, it requires active communication, active coaching. Don't assume or hope that things will be done. Work with your people to achieve results. This requires our next "C"—**COACHING**.

STEP 4: BECOME AN EFFECTIVE COACH

Coaching and communication are obviously linked. Good coaching requires the balanced approach to communication discussed above. Coaching is simply letting someone know that his or her behavior matters to you. We have seen good models of coaches and bad models of coaches. Coaches who were effective in one situation, but not another, effective with one team, but not another. On our televisions we have seen coaches rant, rave, berate and throw chairs, and we have seen coaches quietly take a player aside to re-direct, recognize, and encourage.

It might work with basketball or football players, but ranting and raving does not work with today's workforce, holding to a standard, yes, berating, no.

In any given situation where you see someone doing something you have four options: you can praise and encourage (See Lew Losoncy's book *Turning People On*, InSync Press, 1999), you can tell them what they are doing wrong and provide suggestions on how to improve (re-direct), you can blame, shout and otherwise provide a negative response or you can ignore the behavior totally.

The single most powerful thing you can do to improve employee retention is to use the first of these—PRAISE AND ENCOURAGEMENT. Catch people doing something right and recognize them in the moment with specific and sincere praise. If you do nothing else, if you don't raise salaries, if you don't provide career growth opportunities, if you don't promote them immediately, this strategy alone will help you reduce turnover.

The second best response is re-direction. In hundreds of workshops over the years, I have conducted an exercise called the "Pennies Exercise." It is a discovery exercise that invariably has the same result—people want to grow through re-direction and they do not want to just fumble around until they learn by themselves. Re-direction is just that, it is sending someone off in a slightly different direction. It isn't saying (as I heard a senior vice-president say just last week) "I told you once, how many times do I have to tell you..." It is saying, "I realize that you didn't fully understand what I told you last week, why do you think that happened and what can we do to make sure it doesn't happen in the future."

Or, let's take a tough one. What would I say to redirect the behavior of that vice-president who said "I told you once..."?

First, it has to be done immediately, as close to when you see it as possible, if you wait too long the opportunity is lost.

Second, I would get him off in a quiet place (preferably his office) and describe the behavior that I saw and let the vice-president know that it was not only inappropriate, but frustrating when we are working so hard to reduce turnover. I would say something like...

"Bob, what do you think just happened in your interaction with Steve?"

"I let him know that I won't tolerate that behavior."

"Let me suggest a different view of events. Bob, I just watched you say to Steve, 'I told you once, how many times do I have to tell you...' I am sure this was belittling to Steve, when he walked out of your office his face was pure embarrassment, anger and humiliation. It makes me angry to see one of my v-p's doing this at a time when we are trying to reduce turnover.

I know that you are tired, but I have seen you really help employees to grow in their jobs and I truly believe that you have the ability to be one of the best coaches on the team. Let's continue to focus on that."

That's it. That is re-direction. It is simple and quick, but done with consistency it changes behavior, it makes people aware. It is simply a process of responding to the situation immediately and in private, identifying exactly what you saw and how you feel, and then reinforcing the person for something positive. And, it is doing all of this without blame.

Re-directing is not "natural" for us. What is natural is to get angry and yell or to ignore it all together. But re-direction is a much more effective response, it sends four messages: first, that the behavior observed is not acceptable; second, why it is not acceptable; third, your feelings about the behavior (not the individual) and fourth, that the individual being re-directed has self worth even though the behavior was inappropriate.

Recognition has many of the same steps as re-direction. When you recognize someone you simply find them doing something right and specifically and sincerely acknowledge it.

For example, let's say that an administrative assistant stays late to make sure a critical project gets out on time and correctly. Sure, she is getting paid, but she doesn't have to do this.

The process is similar to re-direction. Before she leaves find a quiet place and say something like, "Thanks for staying, without you there is no way that this project would have been completed. Your attention to detail and anticipation of what could go wrong saved us hours of work. Thanks again."

That's all you have to do.

The secret to effective coaching, however, isn't in the skill, it is in consistently using the skill. To be an effective coach you must commit to re-directing and recognition on a regular basis. If you do, your people will grow and unwanted turnover will decrease. Incidentally, there are few strategies worse than ignoring behavior. Most people would rather receive negative feedback than no feedback. Managers who provide no feedback, managers who do not share information, managers who ignore excellent, average and poor performance are asking for turnover. Remember: Primitive societies punish people by ostracizing them. They say, for violating our rules you will live in a world of silence—it is one of the worst punishments. Don't create a silent environment in your department, division or company. People will leave.

STEP 5: BECOME A COMPETENT LEADER

The final step is competence. Not the competence that is considered part of being a professional as in accounting, engineering, marketing or legal competence. Rather, the required competence is management and leadership competence.

This means that you commit to growing in both the skills of management (organizing, planning, budgeting) and leadership (influencing, communicating, coaching, developing character). Your goal is to become unconsciously competent, to have the skills so well developed that you automatically respond in any situation that requires management or leadership skills.

You do this by practicing and evaluating. At the end of the day, look back and ask yourself:

HOW OFTEN DID I PRAISE?

HOW OFTEN DID I RE-DIRECT?

HOW OFTEN DID I LISTEN, ASK, TELL?

Then, how well did you implement these skills? Did you miss any obvious opportunities? Did you fail to act when you know you should have acted, but just didn't want to? What will you do differently next time?

Next, looking ahead to tomorrow, what opportunities do you think you will have to coach and communicate? What can you do to prepare?

Finally, write it down. Keep a log of how well you are doing. Keep it in your planner, on your PC, in your Palm Pilot, in a journal. Five to ten minutes a day will make you your own coach and enable you to become that leader people want to work with: the unconsciously competent leader.

SUMMARY

It is often said that, "If you keep doing, what you're doing, you will keep getting what you're getting." So how do you change? How do you become more effective as a leader, how do you reduce turnover with the Five C's? Change is complex. I am going to assume that you truly want to make that change and that you are just looking for a tool to help you get there, some details on what I have suggested above. So you simply make yourself a little weekly matrix that will build on the daily planning that you are using.

Place the names of those you supervise and/or want to influence down the vertical, the "Five C's" across the top. If you use a paper planner, put it at the beginning of the week, if electronic, place where you can easily access daily. If you don't use a planner use a yellow pad or some kind of log. But the only way to ensure that you are using these tools is to track your progress. So, every time you communicate, show you care, demonstrate competence, every time you coach an employee or lead with character, give yourself a big check by the name of the person you used it with. Review your journal daily and update your matrix weekly. You will find that this is self-reinforcing and it works. Check your progress at the end of each week against how you would like to be doing. Remember: That which gets measured, gets managed. Get in the habit of using the Five C's and watch your retention improve.

GOOD HIRING DECISIONS AND CAREFUL MANAGEMENT IMPACT RETENTION

By Carol A. Hacker

OVERVIEW

It is one of those little rules that is so obvious that it is often ignored. Turnover begins with the hiring process. If you don't hire well, you increase the likelihood that your turnover will be high. If you look for "bodies" instead of the right (not perfect) fit, you are adding costs to the employee retention process. Retention is much like any other process, if you start with high quality incoming materials, your chances of a high quality product is very good. In this chapter Carol Hacker shows the importance of selecting the right individual and carefully managing that individual in order to reduce turnover.

INTRODUCTION

It's no secret that bad hiring decisions jeopardize profits and impact retention. Do you ever find yourself frustrated with or disappointed in the people you've hired? Hiring is one of the most critical factors associated with employee turnover. The U.S. Department of Labor estimates a bad hiring decision equals 30% of the first year's potential earnings. Worse, if the mistake isn't corrected within a few months, costs increase. Some of the expenses associated with hiring the wrong person include:

- training a replacement;

- advertising;

- the interviewer's time;

- possible unemployment compensation claim;

- potential lawsuit;

- low morale;

- potential customer loss;

- lower productivity;

- recruitment agency fees.

TWO CRITICAL STEPS TO GOOD HIRING DECISIONS

First—Ask. Job interviews measure comprehension, determination, confidence, socialization, self-expression, sense of humor, and persuasiveness. What about skills? You must find out if candidates can do what they claim they can do. Some people inflate their credentials or "talk a good story." Here's a method to determine if candidates can do what they claim they can do. If the candidate says he knows how to prepare a budget, ask him to tell you in as much detail as he can how he's done it in the past. If the candidate claims she's developed a marketing plan, ask her to describe, step by step, how she's done it. Only people who've actually done what they claim will be able to tell you how. It's difficult to fake it; if you know the job for which you're interviewing prospective employees, you will be able to spot a phony quite easily.

Second—Listen. The number one mistake hiring managers make is talking too much. Remember that the primary purpose of a hiring interview is to gather information rather than give information. Think of the 80/20 rule. Speak 20% and listen 80%. Only after you've asked the questions you want answered should you answer the candidate's questions. Remember that when you volunteer too much information as you begin the interview you allow the candidate the opportunity to tell you what you want to hear.

Make the right hiring decisions and you'll improve the morale in your organization too. Managers often seem surprised when I suggest ways to improve morale. Some ask, "What's the big deal about morale? People should be happy to have a job." Here's why it's important. Morale is linked to profit, efficiency, quality, cooperation, productivity, and financial competitiveness. Several factors that impact morale are:

- 👍 attitude toward change;

- 👍 consensus on business goals;

- 👍 rewards and punishment;

- 👍 communication;

- 👍 market and customer orientation;

- 👍 team pride;

- 👍 hiring decisions;

- 👍 the way difficult employees are managed.

DEAL WITH TROUBLE AS A COACH

Suppose you have productive but difficult employees. Disruption affects morale and employee retention, so study uncooperative employees as you would any issue. In addition, consider yourself to be in a relationship with your employees. Managers and supervisors share responsibility for the successes and failures of their people. Coach your staff, when problems arise, with these steps in mind: First, assess problems that are serious enough to require action. Second, solve the most disruptive problems first: prioritize, decide, then act. Third, expect resistance when coaching a poor performer. Be accurate, impartial, and clear about expectations. To the degree that people know what you expect, to the same degree they can succeed. Don't leave them guessing. Fourth, follow up. Many people continue old habits. Encourage and reward progress. Remember that it takes time to change a habit; it's not going to happen overnight.

TREAT EMPLOYEES AS PARTNERS

You can influence retention when you involve your staff in the reasons behind business decisions. Motivated and informed employees eagerly serve their customers. Schedule "Zest" Events. Robert Schaffer, in an article in the New York Times, wrote about "zest factors" which create high energy and motivation. They are:

- 👍 a collaborative mode;

- 👍 a genuine sense of fun and excitement.

- 👍 a clear and compelling goal;

- 👍 success within reasonable grasp;

It's impossible to maintain a continuous motivational environment, but if you use Schaffer's factors to create special events throughout the year you can reduce employee turnover. Because special events improve profitability, reduce waste or increase productivity, in most cases, they're worth the money you spend.

MODIFY WORK

Repetitive work is often boring, but you can make it more interesting. For example, expand a repetitive task to include the complete project from beginning to end. On another job, assign employees to teams where they complement other team members. If you positively change the nature of the assignment you'll discover more enthusiastic people. Work modification uses a variety of skills and increases the employee's autonomy. In addition, most people want to feel empowered by their supervisor. Keep in mind that employees aren't disposable assets. The investment of your time and effort to plan and implement hiring practices, and to improve employee morale, can produce positive results for both the human and financial factors in your organization.

RECRUITING AND RETAINING "GENERATION Y AND X" EMPLOYEES

By Carol A. Hacker

OVERVIEW

The largest group of potential workers in the market today is not "boomers," but the "Generation X" group. Generation Y will shortly outnumber both. So, what do you do to recruit and retain these employees? This chapter provides the why and how of recruiting and retaining "Generation X and Y" employees.

INTRODUCTION

Does your business rely heavily on the younger generation for employees? Are many of your workers in their teens, twenties, and early-to-mid thirties? If so, they're part of Generation Y (born in the 80's) or Generation X (those born between 1964-1982). Many employers would agree that both groups seem to be more motivated by personal fulfillment opportunities on the job than by traditional monetary rewards.

Generation Y employees in particular are viewed as idealistic, with a high level of social consciousness. They're frequently anti-establishment and are concerned about stress on the job among other things. Generally outspoken, they make up the largest pool of young people in the job market today. Promises of overtime pay may not interest them as much as time off to attend a party, concert or just hang out with their friends.

At the risk of lumping everyone into one group, members of Generation X aren't easy to motivate either. There are 44 million of them as opposed to the predicted 78 million in the Y Generation. They have a social conscience; some are vegetarians and consider themselves "free spirits". They traditionally have demanded benefits and time off for recreation. You may see less body piercing and tattoos among this group as they gradually move to a more clean-cut look. They're a resource managers have to rely upon to get the job done, especially for minimum wage-type positions.

The challenge lies in recruiting people from all generations and successfully leading a winning team. There are many ways to go about it. Some of the following suggestions for finding and keeping Generation Y and Generation X employees can also be applied to people of all ages from all backgrounds. How then, does the manager make the connection between the available work force, whether young or old, and meeting the needs of managing the department?

SEARCH FOR NEW HIRES

Begin by asking current employees for recommendations. Encourage employees to recruit friends and family members. "You may want to offer a cash reward to those whose recruits stay for 90 days or longer." One company offers a pair of Nike shoes to employees who stay at least 6 months. They found this strategy to be especially appealing to teens and young adults. Unsolicited applications and resumes are another source. When people stop by your business seeking employment, have them complete an application even if you don't have any vacancies. Prospects that take the time to visit you in person are usually more motivated than someone who makes a phone call. Keep these applications and resumes on file and refer to them when an opening occurs. A phone call to determine the applicant's current status or interest takes only a few minutes.

Former employees can provide a valuable pool of experienced workers, especially when you need help during a seasonal rush. Students home from college for the summer/holidays often want to earn extra cash and they're already trained.

Your customers are a source of potential employees, too. Have flyers available with information about openings and what your business has to offer. Most people want to know what's in it for them. Consider recruiting students from work-study programs. Get proactive in the community. Why not become a member of the advisory committee that supports the vocational education program at the local high school? The program requires students to attend school and work 15 to 20 hours per week. If you work in the retail business, keep an eye open for customer-focused people who work in similar businesses. For example, you might approach prospective employees as one manager does with a card that says, 'You've got a great smile.' If you are dissatisfied or looking for another job, I'd like the opportunity to talk to you." Of course, your recruiting efforts will vary according to the area you operate in, and whether you're a large corporation or a single, privately-held small business.

In your search for employees, find out what other companies offer for pay and benefits. If your pay scale isn't quite as competitive as you'd like, remember that items like schedule flexibility, opportunities to learn new skills, and number of hours worked are important to many prospective employees. Auto liability insurance, free meals and uniforms, paid vacations and holidays and a sign-on bonus are other perks that attract employees of all ages.

GET THE MESSAGE OUT

Newspaper advertising is another way to attract applicants, but may cost more than you want to spend unless you have several vacancies to fill. For example, a company in a larger metropolitan area may find it is cost effective to list several job openings in the same ad for positions in different restaurant or store locations throughout the city. Recruiting via the internet attracts a large audience, especially those of Generation X and Y, as they grew up using computers and are quick to search for job opportunities there.

SCREEN CANDIDATES

The application provides the initial information on a candidate. The face-to-face interview is the next important step. Briefly meeting people when they drop off an application or resume is not the same as a personal interview. Schedule a formal interview with those applicants who seem to be a good fit based upon their credentials. In conducting interviews, keep in mind that some members of the younger generation express their individualism through their manner of dress. Some applicants feel, "This is the way I am, take it or leave it, I'm not changing for the job." What's acceptable varies according to region of the country and type of employer. Workers with multiple earrings, nose rings, or spiked, purple hair may not raise an eyebrow among customers in one area, but result in a decline in business in a more conservative community. Managers have to decide how much is "too much." Make sure the applicant understands your business' guidelines before you hire. Also be aware of how you communicate guidelines. For example, "Our policy doesn't allow our employees to wear nose rings; would you be willing to conform to that policy?" may get a better response than a blunt, "You can't wear those things if you work here; you look like a freak."

KEEP THEM HAPPY

Family members often provide the employee core for family-owned businesses. In such cases, the employees are loyal and turnover is less of a problem. But what can smaller businesses without a core of family employees do to keep good people? A recent national survey found that one of the most common reasons employees leave is they don't feel appreciated. So, don't give feedback to employees only when you're unhappy about something. Take time to notice and comment on their successful efforts. Those who receive recognition for what they did right can more readily accept and benefit from comments about areas that need improvement. Just because your employees are young doesn't mean they don't want respect, courteous treatment, and positive feedback. For example, in one family-owned business the owners said: "We try to recognize employees' birthdays by giving them a card with a gift certificate or cash. It makes them feel special because we made the effort to remember them. It's not how much it cost, but the fact that we are doing something that shows we care." In a business where your employees are required to wear uniforms, do you periodically have days where employees suggest the theme and wear costumes? For example, on "disco day" one company plays disco music and everyone dresses accordingly. Would you consider a 'non-uniform' day and a 'jeans day' once a month?" One company has "gangster days" and employees dress in roaring twenties attire. They've also had "Hawaiian days" and "clown days." Make the workplace fun. Hold a contest to see what department, or in one case, which Call Center makes the fewest mistakes and award cash and prizes. One manager holds an "up sell contest." For example, the employee who sells the most extra pizza cheese topping in a month wins $100." However, he was quick to say that money, as a prize can be short-lived. "I try to reward them when they least expect it." Other ideas for recognizing and rewarding good employees include:

- 👍 Giving away movie passes.

- 👍 Having seven days of special activities and calling it "Employee Recognition Week."

- 👍 Giving a certificate for a free video rental.

- 👍 Awarding a certificate for a CD exchange store.

- 👍 Paying someone to type the employee's term paper.

- 👍 Giving a delivery driver a free tank of gas or oil change.

- 👍 Putting a write-up and/or photograph of employees in the company newsletter.

- 👍 Reserving a bowling alley for an evening, and inviting employees to bowl, karaoke, or simply relax.

- 👍 Letting employees wear their school colors to kick off the football season.

- 👍 Having employees put their ideas on how to do things better into an idea book.

- 👍 Holding a crazy shoelace, funky hat, or ugly tie day.

- 👍 Lending money through a formal, interest-free loan program.

☝ Appealing to your employees' idealism by sponsoring a group project to benefit others in the community.

MAINTAIN A STABLE WORK ENVIRONMENT

Job satisfaction has a direct link to the work environment. In an industry where employees may depend on tips for part of their income, help them have a good attitude about their work in order to increase those tips. Encourage an employee who's working hard to keep a room full of customers happy. The servers usually bear the brunt of the customers' dissatisfaction whether or not they're to blame. If you own a restaurant and deliver food, provide up-to-date maps and make sure new drivers are familiar with the area and have sufficient change before you send them out. This not only helps your employees do a better job and feel more confident, but also provides benefits in terms of customer satisfaction. Be fair about work schedules, particularly if you have family members as part of your staff. All members of the work force deserve equal treatment. Don't assign a non-family-member employee all of the undesirable shifts or work unless you want a lot of employee turnover. Take time to provide orientation for new employees. For many from the Y Generation, this may be their first job. Make sure they understand what you want from them. To quote the late behavioral psychologist, Kurt Einstein, "To the degree that people know what you expect, to the same degree they can succeed." Providing a stable work environment includes personally thanking employees for their efforts, writing notes of appreciation, promoting capable employees, and giving praise in public as well as in private. Hold employee meetings to discuss issues they're concerned about as well as those about which you have concerns. Give them a chance to share their ideas, and listen to what they have to say. Studies have shown that the top motivating techniques are those initiated by the manager and based on employee performance.

SUMMARY

The secret is not only how to find good people, but how to keep them. People work for more than the money, especially the X and Y Generation. It's important to help employees enjoy their jobs. You can accomplish this by setting high standards and making sure employees know what you expect. Create a partnership with your team. Give them a chance to grow and learn new skills; reward their efforts, and celebrate their successes.

GIVING CRITICAL FEEDBACK WITHOUT CAUSING DEFENSIVENESS

By Carol A. Hacker

OVERVIEW

We know that one of the key determinants of whether employees stay with a company or leave that company is how their supervisors treat them—particularly in terms of corrective behaviors. These corrective behaviors can take the form of redirecting poor performance or recognizing outstanding performance. In this chapter, Carol Hacker provides some practical "do's and don'ts" when you must provide critical feedback.

INTRODUCTION

You're a manager in a busy call center in a telecommunications company. Your employees are burned out and sometimes are short-tempered on the phone with customers. You've reprimanded many times but your words seem to have fallen on deaf ears. What's the best way to give critical feedback to these employees?

It's Friday night. Customers are standing six-deep at the hostess station. The phone rings repeatedly with orders for carryouts and deliveries. You already feel like you're losing your mind when two employees call in sick at the last minute! Then a customer asks to see the manager (that's you). He complains that his waitress was rude when he told her his food was burned. You're not surprised because you have witnessed her sharp tongue in the past. This not so-unfamiliar scene needs to be addressed. What would you do?

Most managers have experienced situations similar to the above. You want to keep the customer happy and help the employee learn how to handle such situations without losing his or her temper, and possibly losing a customer as well. She's a steady worker who sometimes loses her cool. He feels the pressure just as you do. You don't want him to quit, but his behavior can be a problem at times. How do you give feedback to the employee without causing more problems?

The goal of feedback is to help employees understand what they did wrong, receive recognition for what they did right and learn the correct way to handle difficult situations as well as increase their desire to improve. Following some basic guidelines can help you give feedback effectively.

First, don't interrogate or reprimand employees in front of other employees or customers. Your goal is to help them improve, not to belittle or embarrass them. Although most managers know this rule, it's often forgotten when the pressure is on. Stay calm. Avoid "adult temper tantrums," the term one employee used to describe her supervisor. "She went nuts when things got tense. The employees feared her constant critical feedback of them as well as her erratic outbursts. She never let up. We decided she was crazy and one day six of us walked off the job at the same time." Choose the right time and the right place to give feedback. A very minor problem may need only a few minutes of private discussion in a quiet corner. Or you may need to schedule a time when you and the employee can sit down in your office for a more intensive talk. It may help to choose a neutral area for the discussion, particularly if an employee is very upset or angry. Don't, however, be like the supervisor who had an electric garage door opener attached to the door of his office. "It was scary," said one of his employees. "He'd call us in, the door would close, and he would blow his top! I finally quit. I couldn't stand the stress."

When you talk with the employee, keep these points in mind. Don't use "always" or "never" in describing their actions. These are unrealistic generalizations, and the employee will usually be able to immediately provide an example to prove you wrong. Don't start with a positive and then immediately switch to a negative. Avoid using "but" as part of your comments, i.e., "You're a good waitress, but..." The "but" negates whatever you said at the beginning and employees quickly learn to react to any compliment as merely the preamble to a criticism. Get to the point. Then conclude with what the employee does well. Don't verbally attack the employee. This can result in a defensive attitude by the employee whose focus shifts from hearing what you have to say to defending his or her actions; it's a natural response. One manager was so insensitive that at one time he stopped speaking to his employees after he verbally abused them. He ignored them and expected the people who worked for him to smooth things over. It didn't work.

Do remember that you and the employee have different perspectives. For example, the customer told you the server was rude after he mentioned the burned food. However, he didn't mention the crude and demeaning manner in which he first spoke to the server. Be sure you get both sides of the story. Do give specific feedback and target specific behaviors. A general statement such as, "I don't like your attitude," doesn't supply enough information. What is it about the employee's attitude that you want changed? Do let the employee know the consequences for inappropriate and unacceptable behavior. Tell employees what they can expect if matters don't improve. Take time to learn how to give feedback appropriately and avoid a situation like the following. "The employee hated his manager.... he sabotaged the operation every chance we got... The manager had no business being in charge of a group of people, much less owning a business. Even his customers grew to dislike him because of the way he treated his employees." Hopefully, most managers will use an approach more like that of this manager. He said, "Persuading people that they are part of the problem is only half the battle. Getting them to change is another factor. I held 'improvement discussions' and always focused on the problem, not the employee as a person. If the employee was interested in continuing employment with me, together we developed an action plan for improvement."

In summary, criticism facilitates growth. It can increase employee morale and retention. If used properly, criticism is used to encourage improvement, not to remind people of failure. The ability to give and take criticism is something every manager must strive to do well.

THE "SOUL" SECRET
TO EMPLOYEE
RETENTION!

By Lew Losoncy, Ed.D.

OVERVIEW

In Chapter 2 Dr. Don Sanders discussed the importance of being a caring leader in order to retain your most valued employees. In this chapter, Dr. Lew Losoncy takes this concept to the next logical step—the essence of seeing the employee not as a project manager, a foreman or an administrative assistant, but as a complex individual with needs that should be carefully addressed if you are to truly increase the retention of critical employees. While Lew addresses the needs of all employees, much of what he has written of in this chapter applies particularly to the young and the aware.

INTRODUCTION

Understanding employee retention involves understanding people's needs. People are moved, or motivated, and thus successfully retained, when a company makes a commitment and takes actions towards the fulfillment of its employees many needs. It's easy to think of a person's financial needs as the sole need the person has that the workplace addresses. It is true that a person, more often than not, takes a job for money. However, everyday experiences tells us that many people are unhappy at work, and also that many leave their jobs for reasons related to non-financial needs not being met.

"They couldn't pay me enough to go back to that demoralizing job!"

"Sure I took a pay cut to work at Imperial. But my first day there I got more pats on the back than I did in 5 years at Eastern."

"When you don't feel yourself growing or going anywhere, you leave."

"If they just asked any of us on the line how to make the job better, and save the company money, we could have showed them dozens of ways. But they don't care, and neither did we."

We could go on and on with stories of why people left their "jobs." And so, we bet, could you. People not only have (1) financial needs, but they have (2) psychological needs, like security and self-esteem, (3) social needs, such as the need for attention, belonging and contributing, (4) professional growth needs, including learning new skills, creativity and advancing on the job, and (5) inspirational needs, and insoulational needs, like finding deeper inspiration, meaning and purpose in the soul of their work.

A TOTAL MOTIVATIONAL STRATEGY FOR THE "SOUL" PURPOSE OF RETENTION

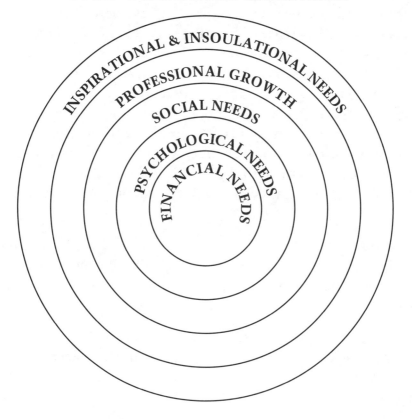

There are many consultants and writers who have looked at the financial and professional needs of the employee as it relates to retention. Few have taken the opportunity to look at the whole person. This chapter does that; it looks at the whole person, or, as I prefer to call it, the "soul" person.

VIEWING THE ORGANIZATION AS A COMMUNITY (COME-UNITY) FOR INDIVIDUALS

An organization determined to dramatically increase retention rates begins by sensing and addressing the total needs of an employee. In this paper, I will start by centering on the "soul" needs of the person at work. Later, I will detail 10 sources of deeper purpose that go beyond the job description that a supervisor, or any leader can focus on for the purpose of building greater meaning for the team members. This chapter differs from some others in this book in that it is "paradigm busting." For many readers it may seem too innovative, too "far out." But I contend (and have the support to show) that when you put soul into a job, you reduce turnover. It has often been said that yesterday's solutions will not solve today's problems. We have a new workforce and they bring a different sense of work with them to the job. The ideas in this chapter speak directly to the issues they raise and the reasons they give for leaving the job.

As a manager, begin by thinking of your organization as a community of which each employee is a contributing member. Morale is clearly related to an individual feeling a part of something bigger than him or her self.

In *Creating Espirit de Corps*, contributor Jim Channon writes sensitively about the organization as community designed to fulfill not only the financial, but also the spiritual needs of its members. Channon observes:

> *When people had tribes to go home to, or villages where they could share their seasonal festival, or even neighborhoods with some personal intimacy, these more spirit evoking elements of culture were part of a natural order of life. But today, our business cultures have become our tribes, our villages and our neighborhoods. They are the building blocks, which will shape our planetary culture. Our older social cultures have become atomized by communications technology and commuting and have largely disappeared as a consequence. So, if there is no*

experience of spirit in corporations, there may not be much spirit in civilization at large.

Is your organization a spirit-evoker, or a spirit destroyer?

TECHNOLOGY AND SOUL

Decades ago psychiatrist Erich Fromm foresaw the implications of technology on the human spirit. Were dehumanization and alienation inevitable in a world where people are reduced to numbers? Fromm concluded that our major task was to humanize our technological world. Perhaps this is part of the soul secret to retention.

In *Care of the Soul*, Thomas Moore provides the reader with a deeper view about the relationship between work and soul. Moore writes:

> *We move closer to the soul's work when we go deeper than intellectual abstraction and imaginary fancies that do not well up from the more profound roots of feeling. The more deeply our work stirs imagination and corresponds to images that lie there at the bedrock of identity and fate, the more it will have soul. Work is an attempt to find an adequate alchemy that both wakes and satisfies the very root of being. Most of us put a great deal of time into work, not only because we have to work so many hours to make a living, but because work is central to the soul's opus.*

MEANING=RETENTION

This article on employee retention is the journey from the skin to the heart of the job, from the job description, inward to the very

soul or our work. The goal is to offer your employees more benefits, more reasons, and deeper, more personal and inspirational and
insoulational purposes to go to work today. Inner meaning that will
last even longer than money or external praise. Since it is meaning
in the soul of our job, one might say it is "relatively" everlasting.

It has been said that finding meaning, even delight in our work,
is the real secret to life. Thoreau concluded that the highest of arts
was found in our awareness that we can actually affect the quality
of our day. After all, when we perceive our experiences differently,
we have different experiences, don't we? As we dig deeper and place
our experiences under the clear microscope of our soul, we see
something, not only different, but something fuller, richer and
more real. Even at work, we can find more, and feel more, by
becoming more aware of the panorama of possibilities on our work-
bench, in front of us, in each moment.

Psychiatrist Carl Jung enlightened us about the solid, accessible
positioning of our soul. Jung expanded our awareness of our range
of resources by pointing out that when we look higher, we find our
spirit; when we dig deeper inside us, we find our soul. Soul is not
"up there." My soul is down here with me, now, on line 5!

Robert Fulghum, in *Pay Attention* de-mystifies soul in his practical observation: "Soul is found in the quality of what I am doing.
If my activities are deep in meaning, then they are rich in soul, and
so am I. Thus, for me, nourishing the soul means making sure I
attend to those things to give my life richness and meaning."

Rabbi Harold Kushner in *God's Fingerprints On Our Souls*
brings our soul closer to us as he concludes:

> *"When your life is filled with the desire to see the
> holiness (wholeness, our word) in everyday life,
> something magical happens: ordinary life becomes
> extraordinary, and the very process of life begins to
> nourish your soul!"*

And of course, we add. Even at work!

The Beatles, in their song, *Hey Jude* told us that all the movement we need is on our shoulders. And that our task in life is to take a sad song and make it better. And, may we add, especially after A Hard Day's Night at work! In a way, soul music!

IF SOMEONE FINDS BURIED TREASURE, IT MEANS THAT IT MUST BE THERE

As a psychotherapist to the workplace, I wanted to help people develop personal motivational tools to dig into the deeper meaning of their work. After all, the workplace is about people. The passion, fire, energy and life in the workplace is in the minds and the hearts of the workers. I believe that companies can do much to provide incentives to employees, to make the workplace hassle and harassment free, safer and environmentally more pleasant. But I wanted to go even farther for the purpose of helping people find more meaning in their work, so they would stay.

Too many people aren't finding meaning and fulfillment in their daily jobs. Then they take off to find it somewhere else! Many are negatively affected by work. In fact, Mihaly Csikszentmibaly concluded in his brilliant work, *Finding Flow* that people endorse an item that reads, "I wish I was doing something different" when they are at work more than at any other time during the day. Not a shock to any of us, but must it be that way?

"My soul is down here with me, now, on line 5!"

This is unfortunate because if some people find buried treasure, that is proof that the riches must be there. Some people find the soul in their jobs, while others, on the same job, have to "go to work" instead. Consider the following levels of meaning found by some people on the job:

- Some people are in a rut, robotically stagnating through each day, while others on the same job, as they look deeper into the soul of their work, are finding the personal growth they are gaining on the job. (Personal Meaning)

- Some people aren't noticing their own accomplishments, like mastering of difficult tasks, correcting, improving, solving problems, while others on the same work are finding, as they look deeper into the soul of their job, task meaning and skill development. (Task Meaning)

- Some people are going through the motions at work, while others on the same job are finding, as they look deeper into the soul of their work, the potential to master their roles, experiencing career or professional growth and are seeing advancement. (Career, Professional Meaning)

- Some people are going to work, isolating themselves, never interacting, seeing other departments as "the enemy," while others on the very same job are finding, as they look deeper into the soul of their work, rewarding relationships, belonging and contributing, as well as understanding the whole company. (Social Meaning)

- Many people are working within a team with whom they feel no connection, while others on the same job, as they look deeper into the soul of their work, experience the power of open communications, mutual progress and shared dreams together. (Team Meaning)

- Some people are going to their job, viewing the "company" or viewing "labor" as "them" on the other side, while others on the same job are finding in the soul of their work, the rewards of contributing to fulfill a collective vision, being a part of a dynamic culture, and being a stakeholder. (Organizational Meaning)

- Many people are going to work and are relating to the customer as a thing, thereby making their own work unimportant because they work with things, while others on the same job are finding in the soul of their work an own important connection to the person who is called a customer. (Customer Meaning)

- Some people are going to work, doing their jobs and going home, never recognizing their role in their community, while others on the same job are finding in the soul of their work, that they can contribute to making their own community a better place. (Community Meaning)

- Many people are going to work each day throughout their whole life and never feeling they are building a better world, yet others on the same job are looking deeper into the soul of their work and realizing that they are changing the world. (World Meaning)

- Most people are going to work and never feeling any inspiration, while others on the same job are finding in the soul of their work a direct route to their own fulfillment, passion and even an expressway to their God. (Inspirational Meaning)

We wrote to encourage people at all levels in organizations, to plug into this independent energy source of inner motivation that we saw the most successful and fulfilled workers do. We couldn't imagine a more important mission than to help people find the already existing soul in their jobs. Many haven't.

Consider the findings of an expert on work. Studs Terkel wrote in *Working,* his cross-sectional research on peoples' attitudes towards their jobs,:

> *It (work) is about a search for daily meaning, as well as daily bread, for recognition, as well as for cash, for astonishment, rather than torpor; in short, for a sort of life, rather than a Monday through Friday sort of dying. Perhaps immortality, too, is part of the quest. To be remembered, spoken or unspoken, was the wish of the heroes and heroines of this book.*

> *There are, of course, the happy few who find a savor in their daily job: the Indiana stonemason who looks upon his work and sees it is good; the Chicago piano tuner who seeks and finds the sounds that delights; the bookbinder who saves a piece of history; the Brooklyn fireman who saves a piece of life...But don't these satisfactions tell us more about a person than about his task? Perhaps. Nonetheless, there is a common attribute here: a meaning to their work well over and beyond the reward of the paycheck.*

THEY FOUND THE SOUL IN THEIR JOBS.

David Whyte wrote in *The Heart Aroused:*

> *Work is slowly mastered. The soul life of a person is always larger and greater the more we come to know it. We go to work. But it is our soul we put into it. Work is a series of events. The soul, as James Hillman says, turns those workaday events into an experience.*

Whyte optimistically concludes:

> *Whatever we choose to do, the stakes are very high.*
> *With a little more care, a little more courage, and*
> *above all, a little more soul, our lives can be so eas-*
> *ily discovered and celebrated in work and not, as*
> *now, squandered and lost to its shadow.*

There is soul in every job, whether we find it or not! Take our favorite waitress: Leona, the bubbling 72 year-old waitress is the inspiration to her Seafood restaurant team. Another waitress even describes Leona as her hero. The barmaid's eyes beam when she describes Leona's caring for people at work. Customers ask for Leona. Leona simply loves her work. She comes to life as she animates while enthusiastically recommending this or that special. She delivers the smoking garlic bread with an envious look. She literally touches her heart and looks up to the heavens when her customers comment on the great tasting food. Leona remembers our name, and our previous order, 12 years earlier at our last stop. One day we learned how miraculous her attitude really is. Another employee explained that Leona recently lost her husband and years before, two of her sons in separate accidents.

There are millions of waiters and waitresses around the world who put the same amount of work time into their jobs. Their bodies are present, but because they haven't found the depth of opportunities in the soul of their work, their day is long, their meaning and contribution to the world is nil, and their rewards for their efforts appear only once every two weeks. One third of their life, the part at work, is lived less fully, less creatively and both quality time, and potential, are lost.

What does Leona know, think, feel, see or do or sense that others, who are alienated, discouraged, dispirited or have lost their soul miss?

How much would it be worth for you as a worker to find what Leona found?

How much would it be worth for you as a leader to be able to help your people to find the soul in their jobs?

Could there be a more important mission at work?

OUR SOUL HAS A DEEPER SENSE OF THINGS

In his bestseller, *Seat of the Soul*, Gary Zukav contrasts the deeper view the multi-sensory soul has with the surface view of the personality that is handcuffed by the five senses:

> *Only the personality can judge, manipulate and exploit. Only the personality can pursue external power. The personality can also be loving, compassionate and wise in its relationships with others, but love, compassion and wisdom do not come from the personality. They are experiences of the soul.*

Your soul is that part of you that is immortal. Every person has a soul, but a personality that is limited in its perception of the five senses is not aware of its soul and therefore cannot recognize the influences of its soul. As personality becomes multi-sensory, its intuitions, its hunches and subtle feelings become important to it. It senses things about itself, other people and situations in which it finds itself that it cannot justify on the basis of the information that its five senses can provide. It comes to recognize intentions, and to respond to them, rather than the actions and the words that it encounters. It can recognize, for example, a warm heart beneath a harsh and angry manner, and a cold heart beneath polished words.

Leona cultivates her soul, and in the process finds the soul in her job. So many others, guided by personality, limited by five-sense awareness, miss the dimension of fuller human expression. Zukav argues that just as we know that the visual sense can grasp the colors of the rainbow, but cannot reach the extra-sensory ranges of ultraviolet or infrared, our soul fills in the gaps of what we intuitively "know" exists, but can't sensually "see." The expanded awareness, you might say the "infrared" and the "ultraviolet" in the workplace become visible to those who pay attention to their own soul in the workplace. And then those visionaries "see" the soul in their job.

The cost of finding the soul is to pay attention.

Wouldn't it be tragic for our life if there was more meaning to be found in the depth of our soul at work, and we went through our whole lifetime…unaware?

"There is a soul in every job,

whether we are aware of it, or not!"

Lance H.K. Secretan argues in *Reclaiming Higher Ground* that the soul is often missed in the workplace.

Traditional managers dismiss the notion of a workplace with a soul, which I prefer to call a "Sanctuary," believing that this is a role more appropriate for organized religion. This attitude is based upon the misconception that "soft stuff" has no place in the organization. An awesome opportunity awaits those who are tired of the old approach to leadership and who have the courage to blaze a promising new trail.

We have traditionally believed that 'business is business' and that work should not be concerned with the spirit. This belief, however, does not square with the experience of millions of uninspired souls who yearn for a new generation of evolving leaders, who will regenerate our organizations and create the appropriate environment in which our souls will flourish. The evolved individuals who offer a soaring vision of their organization's purpose on this planet will create soulful workplaces-Sanctuaries-that invite employees to bring their souls to work as well as their minds.

The "Sanctuary," or safe view of the workplace was simultaneously, but independently offered as well by another prominent thinker. Lewis Richmond, in his uplifting book, *Work is a Spiritual Practice*, asks us to imagine that our workplace looked differently.

> *Allow your imagination to alter your image of this place. Give it a different roof, the roof of a church or temple. See its architecture as reflecting your spiritual values. Church...*

> *Imagine that a different visual power opens up within you, so as you can see your coworkers, not as they appear on the outside, but as they really are...*

> *Imagine the whole room (or shop floor, or construction site or restaurant kitchen) being lit up by a subtle light. Your coworkers are going about their ordinary tasks, seemingly unaware of the luminosity. But you can see it, because you choose to see it, because you want to see it, as a conscious act of spiritual intention...*

> *See the workplace as holy, and all the people in it as holy. The materialist, the skeptic in us, may whisper: 'This is not the way things REALLY are.' The spiritual life within you responds: 'This is the way things really are, and the ordinary way we see has a veil that hides it from us.'*

> *Remember, it's all in your mind.*

Remember, it's all in your mind. Epictetus, the Stoic philosopher 2,000 years ago proclaimed:

It's not what happens to us in life that affects us; rather it is the way we look at what happens to us that does!

OUR SOULS' EYES "SEE" THINGS THAT OUR FACES' EYES MISS

Our daughter, Gabrielle Losoncy, elaborated on her vision: "Actually, I have four eyes; two on my face and two inside my head. And the two eyes inside my head can see further. If I close my two eyes in my face, I can see anything. Right now I can see two birds in Alabama. But, if I open my eyes in my face and only use them, I can't see Alabama anymore!"

Not a bad vision for a seven year-old. Listen to your child's view of your work when they say, "Neat!"

OUR SOUL "SEES" DEEPER PURPOSES

The story goes each of three men laboring in the field was asked, "What are you doing." The first responded, "I'm earning a living."

The second responded, "I'm tilling the soil."

The third soulfully shouted, "I'm feeding our community."

"Our soul fills in the gaps of what we intuitively 'know' exists,but can't quite see without the help of the soul's clearer microscope."

The following examples from the lives of those who "work with soul" show that it is often just a question of which eyes you choose to use.

OUR SOUL "SEES" WIDER CONNECTIONS

When our friend Jim Belasco, author of *The Flight of the Buffalo* asked a hospital custodian about the nature of his work, he pridefully answered, "I help to save lives around here."

OUR SOUL "SEES" LOVE IN OUR PRODUCTS AND SERVICES

When we spoke to a man on the assembly line, bottling beauty products, he shared his soulful love of his work by explaining, "I love this product. You see, we make it here."

OUR SOUL "SEES" OUR JOB AS A SOURCE OF PERSONAL GROWTH (Male, 26, pharmaceutical sales)

"I look at each day as a tremendous opportunity to not just sell products, but in a deeper way, to build my own self-confidence. I have to speak with MDs and in the beginning, I was intimidated. But now, less than a year later, I have gained in confidence and in sales. Where else can you get paid and grow personally on a job? I sometimes wonder how much my job is really worth to me?"

OUR SOUL "SEES" OUR JOB AS A SOURCE OF SELF-ESTEEM (Female, 49, packer)

"I think of my job as me. When my order is packed perfectly, I right now, am perfect at my job. Kind of like getting a 10.0 in an ice skating event in the World Olympics."

OUR SOUL "SEES" OUR JOB AS A SOURCE OF TEAM PRIDE (The set-up specialists, Pittsburgh resort)

"We can break down and set up any room, any size, any number of chairs in 15 minutes. Everybody at 7 Springs knows us. Tell us there's a change in the way a room is supposed to be laid out, and we only have a few minutes, we are on our beepers to each other and people are coming from all directions. Challenge is what makes our juices flow. We're the best there is."

"Wouldn't it be tragic if there was dramatically more meaning to be found on our jobs, and we went through our whole life...unaware?"

OUR SOUL "SEES" CREATIVE OPPORTUNITIES IN OUR JOB (Female, 55, second grade teacher)

"A lot of children hate math, but love solving problems. So I make math into a mystery. We are looking for "x" which represents the number that committed the crime. The clues are the other numbers in the problem. We eliminate numbers that it couldn't be because the evidence isn't there. And then, we find the solution."

OUR SOUL "SEES" OUR JOB AS A SOURCE OF INSPIRATION (Female, 29, hairdresser)

"No, we don't just do hair. We change peoples' lives in this salon."

May we suggest "Sanctuary" instead of salon?

OUR SOUL "SEES" OUR JOB AS CONTRIBUTING TO OUR COMMUNITY (Female and male partners, builders)

"The greatest satisfaction to our crew is in taking a set of plans, and then building something in that empty lot. And then watching a family come by day after day, seeing our progress, imagining their finished bedrooms, and then moving in. Yeah, we usually deliver the home on time."

OUR SOUL "SEES" OUR JOB AS A POTENTIAL FOR PROBLEM SOLVING (Professional beauty product manufacturing sales team)

"We call ourselves 'The Find-a-Wayers!' We look at every challenge and conclude that somewhere in our collective minds, there is an answer."

OUR SOUL "SEES" OUR JOB AS AN OPPORTUNITY TO EXPERIENCE "FLOW" (Female, 35, secretary, real-estate)

"Sometimes I get lost in my work. I come in, there's a full desk, there are crises throughout the day, and I am moving and moving, getting things done, and I realize that I forgot to take lunch. I am so into what I do, sometimes I forget to even look at my watch. Things just need to get done."

These are samples of the many individuals who are discovering the soul in themselves, and are instantly realizing the soul in their jobs at work. I hope that, in some big way, you might be inspired or insouled by the potential meaning in your present job. In fact, if you get to enjoy and find meaning in your work, you could say that you'll never have to go to work again.

Shortly, we will discuss how finding soul is an inside job, because it is more empowering when it comes from within. However, a sensitive, aware and soulful leader, manager, supervisor or co-worker can help initiate the job-souling process. One such foreman helped me to find the soul in my job.

Mr. U was our foreman as we college students bundled bars of steel during those hot summers from 1964-1967 at the Carpenter Specialty Steel Company. Bundling bars of steel may seem like a boring job to you. It could have been if we missed the soul in the job. Mr. U took some time to bring the soul to the job by making a connection between our tedious work and its eventual contribution to the world. I especially remember one day when Umpy casually commented to me that what I was bundling was destined to be a part of the first United States spacecraft that lands on the moon. I remember literally feeling chills as I bundled that day. Still feel them today decades later. My soul was engaged in my work. And that the job of bundling steel had soul. Can you feel it? Time seemed to stop for me as I lived the significance of the moment

After working one night shift, I was invited by the big boys, the veteran bundlers, to have a few 7 am beers at the Showboat. I told the old timers about the soul filled experience. Two others chimed in, adding other world-wide contributions we Carpenter bundlers make. Soul was added to Soul. One cynic tried to de-soul us by arguing, 'it's nothing more than a job.'

Need I tell you who the most motivated and happy workers were on that job? The ones who found the soul in their job! And I guess I don't have to tell you whose long eight hour day seemed like an eternity.

Anyway I don't know where you were on July 20, 1969, but I was close up to my TV as Neil Armstrong stepped on the moon and proclaimed, 'One small step for a man, one giant leap for mankind.' I was waiting for him to give the list of credits as I imagined him saying, 'And to you Lew Losoncy for bundling those bars of steel, thank you!'

Umpy made a difference. You can too.

"By bringing more of our own soul into our work, we immediately begin seeing hints of the soul in our job."

After bringing your own soul to work, you are encouraged to help your employees to look at their jobs differently. Expand their awareness by embracing each of the ten levels the job's soul touches; (1) personal, (2) task, (3) career or profession, (4) social, (5) team, (6) company, (7) customer, (8) community, (9) world and (10) spirit and soul.

Helping people to seek the quest for the soul in their job is the most important journey of our work life. Maybe our whole life.

FINDING THE SOUL IN OUR JOBS MAY EVEN CHANGE OUR WHOLE LIFE

After all, one-third of our life is at work. Plus, the other two-thirds of our life is affected by our attitude towards our work experiences. Discovering and creating motivating, meaningful, even inspirational ways of viewing the soul in our everyday job, our fellow workers, and our workplace has an immediate positive impact on our whole life. How important is it for us to invest a little time to inspire ourselves for our lives at work?

Well, our view of work affects not just our work, but our whole life. Our view of our daily work affects:

our physical health,

our feelings about ourselves,

our relationships with our significant others,

our children,

and, even perhaps, how long we live

And that's when we are not working!

In the workplace, our view of our work affects:

how long our day feels,

our happiness and fulfillment on the job,

our personal growth,

our relationships with our teammates,

our beliefs about our contribution to society,

our degree of stress,

our potential and promotability,

our income,

our view of the company,

the company's view of us,

our view of our future!

To make our workday and our life have more energy, elation and ecstasy, we have to save the soul in our job.

And that is the "soul" secret to employee retention.

Here are 10 levels of ideas to start your company's retention program with. As a manager or leader ask yourself how you can help your employees find some of these sources of meaning in their lives. If you can, if you can help them see their job as "feeding the community" or "helping to put a man on the moon," your retention issues will be fewer. You may even find yourself with the problem of too many applicants rather than too much turnover.

10 LEVELS TO FIND SOUL IN YOUR JOB

Inspirational Meaning: self-actualization at work, flow, spirit, passion, God at work

World Meaning: building a better world, making a difference on the earth

Community Meaning: contributing to a local or a professional community

Customer Meaning: customer sensitivity, striving for excellence and perfection in products and services, customer humanizing

Organizational Meaning: fulfilling vision, living cultural values, feeling empowered, empowering, identifying with the company's purpose and progress, stakeholding, being the difference in the company

Team Meaning: mutual respect, mutual progress, synergy of ideas, team theming, team victory, open communications, contributing at a team level

Social Meaning: rewarding relationships, attention, belonging, encouraging

Career, Professional Meaning: professional growth, technical skill development, job or role mastery, recognition, advancement

Task Meaning: skill refinement, task mastery over specific tasks, job achievement at a task level, correction, improvement, progress, problem solving

Personal Meaning: personal growth, pride in achievement at a personal level, self-esteem, creativity, security, love, courage, curiosity, challenge

50 MEANING SOURCES FOR OUR WORKLIFE

(In coaching and conversations you can help your employees answer these questions and thus become fully involved in the process of purposeful work.)

PERSONAL MEANING

Personal Growth: How have I grown since I started with our company?

Pride: What accomplishments do I feel most proud about in doing what I do?

Self-Esteem: How has my work changed my belief in myself through the years?

Creativity: Where have I put my own ideas into my work that was meaningful?

Security: What security have I earned through the years on the job?

Love: What do I love most about my job?

Courage: What was my most courageous moment on my job?

Curiosity: How can I use my curiosity to grow even further on my job?

Challenge: What is my biggest challenge today? How can I turn it into a positive as I have done in the best personal growth moments in my past?

Vision: What personal quality will I develop this year?

TASK MEANING

Skill Refinement: What skills have I developed since being here at the company?

Task Mastery over Specific Tasks: What have I learned to master, to really do well? Maybe I am one of the best there is at it!

Task Progress: What area of my work am I most progressing at, perhaps because I've been opened to learn?

Correction: What was a significant moment in which I heard a better way than I was trying, and I corrected myself?

Problem Solving: What problem did our company have that I helped to solve?

Future Improvement: What task do I need to work on to make my future even better?

CAREER, PROFESSIONAL MEANING

Professional Growth: How have I grown, not personally, but professionally since being with our company?

Previous Job Mastery: What previous jobs have I had to learn and master?

Recognition: What recognition have I received for my work?

Advancement: What advancements have I made since I started with our company?

Future Career Advancements: What am I willing to work towards to make my future even better than today?

SOCIAL MEANING

Rewarding Relationships: What rewarding relationships have I found here at our company?

Attention: Who notices me? Who says "hello" or knows things about me, or offers some support when I need it?

Belonging: With which group do I feel I belong?

Contributing: Who have I contributed to help them become better?

Encouraging: Who do I believe in, or have supported?

TEAM MEANING

Mutual Respect: Who on our team do we respect for each other?

Mutual Progress: With whom on our team are we growing together?

Synergy of Ideas: With whom on our team do we brainstorm new ideas together and things just flow?

Team Theming: What makes our team special? How are we unique?

Winning Team: What have we accomplished together?

Open Communications: With whom can I communicate about our work both the good news and bad news? Who can I be extremely honest with for the purpose of making things better?

Contributing at a Team Level: How have I made our team a better place?

ORGANIZATION MEANING

Fulfilling Vision: How am I helping fulfill our company's vision?

Living Cultural Values: Where was an example of when I truly lived out our company's values?

Feeling Empowered: In what areas do I feel the company trusts me to trust my sense? How does it make me feel that I have earned that trust?

Being the Difference: How have I been a difference for our company?

Future Contribution: What could I give, that I know the company needs to make it a better place?

CUSTOMER MEANING

Customer Sensitivity: As I walk a mile in our customer's shoes, what am I most sensitive to?

Striving for Perfection in Services to our Customer: What are some examples where I fought for our customer to give them the best service?

Customer Humanizing: Where have I consciously treated a customer as a unique, special, distinct, important human being, rather than just another customer? Did it work? Could it work more if I did it more?

COMMUNITY MEANING

Community Development: How have I, through my work, made my community a better place?

Professional Community: In what ways have I advanced my profession in our community's eyes?

WORLD MEANING

Building a Better World: What is the single thing that sticks out in my mind as to how I am building a better world?

Touching Lives: How many lives have I touched, directly and indirectly, through my work since being with our company?

INSPIRATIONAL MEANING

Self-Actualizing at Work: Where, in my work, am I moving toward becoming the person I am capable of becoming?

Flow: When am I most myself on the job, or when am I truly "flowing?"

Spirit: What gives me the most satisfaction about my work? What makes my spirit?

Passion: What do I believe in more than anything else about my work?

God at Work: How am I inspiring a better universe and connecting to God, or my equivalent to a God through my work?

SOURCES

Csikszentmihayi, Mihaly. **Finding Flow**. New York: Harper & Row, 1995

Fulgum, Robert. **Pay Attention in Handbook for the Soul**. Toronto: Little Brown, 1995

Kushner, Harold. **God's Fingerprints on the Soul in the Handbook for the Soul**. Toronto: Little Brown, 1995

Losoncy, Lewis. **The Motivating Team Leader**. Boca Raton, Florida: CRC Press, 1995

Losoncy, Lewis. **Turning People On!** Sanford, Florida: InSync Publications, 2000

Losoncy, Lewis. **What Is, Is!** Boca Raton, Florida: CRC Press, 1995

Secretan, Lance. **Reclaiming Higher Ground**. New York: McGraw Hill, 1997

Whyte, David. **The Heart Aroused**. New York: Doubleday, 1995.

Zukav, Gary. **The Seat of the Soul.** New York: Simon and Schuster, 1989

BOTTOM-LINE SPIRITUAL

*The Non-Material Aspects
of Employee Satisfaction*

by David Baker, Ph.D.

OVERVIEW

*When Joel Barker's **The Business of Paradigms** (better known as **"The Paradigm Tape"**) was first introduced in the late 1980's, one of his most surprising findings was that new paradigms are often created by "outsiders." These outsiders, individuals with no vested interest in maintaining systems that are not working to their fullest, have no problem in suggesting different, even radical, solutions to problems. Einstein put it differently when he said that the problems of today cannot be solved by the same type of thinking that created the problems in the first place. Joel Barker would call David Baker a "para-*

digm pioneer," that is, someone with a point of view that is outside mainstream thinking, yet crowded with potential. As you read the following article see it for the opportunity it presents and the concepts that are clarified. When Megatrends was first published over twenty years ago, John Naisbitt wrote that the farther we get into a high tech culture, the more people will need "high touch." David Baker's philosophy of ministry concept takes this "high touch" need of people into direct contact with the line of retention. If your first thought is that this stuff is just too controversial, too soft, too far removed from reality, then you might remember that Dr. Ken Blanchard, best selling author and former CEO of one of the most successful training companies in the country, recently resigned his CEO position to become CSO—Chief Spiritual Officer— the company continues to thrive.

PART 1: INTRODUCTION TO THE CONCEPT OF "BOTTOM-LINE SPIRITUAL"

Spirituality and retaining employees? Spirituality and the profit motive? Spirituality and corporate culture? Strange bedfellows, at best. But, being the forward thinkiing leader you are, you've visited your local Book Warehouse where new volumes are arriving daily heralding how spiritual issues and corporate culture have ended their standoff and are living happily ever after. You've looked at, maybe even read the stuff, and think, nice theory. Don't believe a word of it. And even if a meeting of the minds were possible, it will be a hundred years before it'll be a reality. Let the grandchildren deal with it.

And indeed, you would be justified in your skepticism. Spirituality and the business of retaining your best employees? It's the philosophical equivalent of oil and water. Business and theological suicide. The end of corporate culture as we know it. Actually, that last line just might be true.

And that's what this chapter is about.[1]

Now, since this is a chapter on spirituality, relax, take a deep breath and imagine yourself as, well, yourself. One day, say on the commute home, you find yourself taking your quarterly moment

---

[1] Peter Senge is one of the pioneers of the revolution in new thinking about leadership, organizational learning, innovation, and enhancing the capacity of people to work toward common goals. On the faculty of the Sloan School of Management at MIT, he is perhaps best known for his books, *The Fifth Discipline* and recently, *The Dance Of Change*. The following excerpt is from his scouting report delivered Wednesday, May 24th, 2000 at a conference titled *"Exploring Off The Map,"* hosted by Leadership Network, a consulting and resource organization to churches:

"Leaders of the future are men and women who are keenly aware of the larger context of things. They are not merely focused on the content or the form of things—like technique, procedure, methodology, shape, form or application. These mostly fall into the physical or material plane of reality. These new leaders appreciate the value of the non-physical and non-material aspects of reality, heretofore unexplored for most business people. These folks recognize the value of context—source, intention, integrity, vision, values, and the larger purpose of things. These are the things that mystics talk and write about.

Able to appreciate context, these leaders are also sensitive beyond what they see and hear. They have a keen sixth sense that allows them to discern beyond the physical senses. They can pick up on "texture of the space," like knowing something or someone isn't right without any rational reason. In this way, they are irrational. They are deeply intuitive and can instantly pick up when the texture changes, like a dog behaves just before an earthquake.

These leaders possess a strong knowing that goes beyond mental capacity; this knowing relies on their deep sense of interconnection with others, an appreciation for what philosopher Martin Buber called the "between."

Sound crazy and off-the-edge? If it does, you might look at you own attachment to the status quo … We all have attachments to the way things are you know. It shows up differently in each of us, but we all resist change somehow. That's what makes real transformation so damn difficult."

to look into the depths of your soul. If you're like most, you notice there are at least two of you: the business-minded, cool-headed, strategy-oriented, deal-making, profit-motivated person. And the loving, good-natured, compassionate, helpful, self-sacrificing person—the spiritual person. Heretofore you have happily existed as a schizophrenic, keeping one away from the other for fear of the outbreak of an intra-psychic world war. For example, with regard to this chapter, the all-business side of you might say, "Can anything practical come of such spiritual drivel?" While the spiritual side suggests, "Of course, goodness and peace and compassion ought to be, and therefore can be, integrated in one's daily business tasks. Look at those New England ice cream guys and that actor with the salad dressings. I'm thrilled that yet another writer feels he has something to contribute about this stuff."

With those clearly defined borders in mind, this chapter has three goals: First, and most generally, it seeks to make a contribution to healing the split between our spiritual lives and our work lives. Second, and more specifically, the chapter assumes that healing the split occurs as you risk experimenting with the practical "tools" suggested here. And thirdly, when translated to action, these tools and suggestions provide the most powerful reasons for employees to remain loyal and committed to an enterprise. They are most powerful because they are most human. So much research says that employees are tired of checking their humanity with the receptionist on the way to their desks—and yet, and yet, so many of us continue to ignore the obvious. So, if you choose to read on, I believe you will at least find a few unique and helpful tools to add to your bag of retention tricks. And more than that, you may find the tools so much fun that you might think it worth wrapping an entire department around the philosophy from which they spring. That philosophy I will reluctantly call "spirituality."

What is spirituality? It comes from the Greek word "pneuma," which means breath, moving air, or wind. And like wind, that which is spiritual is real but unseen. That's important. Because we live in a culture that values most that which is most tangible, that which can be seen, measured, or calculated. Spirituality is not religion, ethics, or morality, though they do share things in common. It is not specific to any denomination, religion, or culture, but may be a quality of each. In the true nature of the term it literally transcends the human conceptions and refers to a radically different set of ideas and experiences. With that in mind, and specific to the purposes of this chapter, I offer the following definition of spirituality:

> *Spirituality refers to any activity, event, relationship or environment that is both experienced as "real," and at once beyond the scope of usual human experience.*

In other words, spirituality refers to "transcendent" realities which are vital to sustain life, but which are difficult or impossible to measure in terms of value, worth, or profitability. Things like faith, hope, trust, and appreciation all fall in this category. None are empirically measurable, but all are vital contributors to the success of any business. And, more specifically, they are vital to an employee's sense of well-being.

I am now going to introduce another phrase, which I think will help define more clearly what we are about in our goal of keeping the best employees. For the past fifteen years I have served as a minister in churches in a variety of Protestant denominations. Every church I served had, at least in theory, what was termed a "Philosophy of Ministry." This is roughly equivalent to a mission or purpose statement in the business sector. Churches are largely service organizations that provide contexts for religious expression, teaching and socializing. Churches realize their survival depends on providing service to their members in such a way that they have an experience of the transcendent in worship each week, while they also experience an ever-deepening understanding of their religion's teaching, and an increasing experience that they belong to the community. The first two serve to impart a sense of meaning to life, the third extends a sense of hospitality or a feeling of belonging. Churches see their work as "ministry," which comes from a root word meaning "service."

Since this book is about ways to keep your best employees, I am going to suggest that you take the time to clearly define your philosophy of ministry, or your way of being of service to your employees. This intangible can't compete with a higher salary. In fact, it doesn't need to. It offers something of equal or greater importance appeals to another side of the employee, namely the human side. And that is all too rare in these times. From here on, I will use "Philosophy of Ministry" to describe and to measure how we're doing in creating a business climate that supports and keeps the best employees.

And The Point Is . . . ? You may have a mission statement for your corporation, but do you personally have a philosophy of ministry for your employees? If not, create one (and if you have one, has it been revised to reflect current attitudes and trends?). What should it communicate? How will it reflect both your corporate and spiritual values? What specific language would you use? Developing one will give employees the clear message that you consider their personal well-being a top priority.

How? The rest of this chapter will define several essentials of a good philosophy of ministry, or philosophy of service. It is essentially a "how to" of developing a philosophy of ministry. It'll be up to you to pick and choose those which fit best within your present business philosophy, and to determine which of these have a realistic chance of going beyond mere theory to implementation.

WHY SPIRITUALITY?

Before we get into the what of the philosophy of ministry, let's look a little bit more about the why. Let's begin with the following story. This story is of an American investment banker who was standing at the pier of a small coastal Mexican village when a small boat with just one fisherman docked. Inside the boat were several large yellow fin tuna. The American complimented the Mexican on the quality of his fish and asked how long it took to catch them. The Mexican replied, "Only a little while." The American then asked why didn't he stay out longer and catch more fish. The Mexican said he had enough to support his family's immediate needs. The American then asked, "But what do you do with the rest of your time?" The Mexican fisherman said, "I sleep late, fish a little, play with my children, take siesta with my wife, Maria, stroll into the village each evening where I sip wine and play guitar with my amigos—I have a full and busy life."

The American scoffed, "I have an MBA and could help'you. You should spend more time fishing and with the proceeds, buy a bigger boat. With the proceeds from the bigger boat, you could buy several boats. Eventually you would have a fleet of fishing boats. Instead of selling your catch to a middleman you would sell directly to the processor, eventually opening your own cannery. You would control the product, processing and distribution. You would need to leave this small coastal fishing village and move to Mexico City, then to Los Angeles and eventually to New York City where you will run your expanding enterprise."

The Mexican fisherman asked, "But, how long will this all take?" To which the American replied, "15-20 years." "But what then?", the fisherman inquired. The American laughed and said, "That's the best part. When the time is right you would announce an IPO and sell your company stock to the public and become very rich, you would make millions." "Millions," the fisherman responded. Then what?" The American said, "Then you would retire. Move to a small coastal fishing village where you would sleep late, fish a little, play with your kids, take siesta with your wife, stroll to the village in the evenings where you could sip wine and play your guitar with your amigos." (Thanks to Peter Beloin and his amigo.)

The story illustrates the meeting of two very different minds. The American businessman sees the potential for reaping personal reward by gaining control, power and money, which, in and of themselves, are not bad things. He could make the case that pursuing such ends would be a "spiritual task," in that he and the fisherman would bring a valuable product to market for many more to enjoy. Note, however, that both approaches achieve the same end. The difference is that the businessman believes that spending one's life in pursuit of "more" is better than being satisfied with what is, right now. In fact, the fisherman's seemingly glib satisfaction with his present situation may appear to the businessman as laziness, or as though he has "settled," that he lacks ambition, drive or motivation. From another perspective, the fisherman is content with what is, right now. He has learned the fine art of wanting what he already has.

Put another way, the businessman proceeds from a perspective that there is something the fisherman is lacking, which is true. The fisherman believes he lacks nothing, indeed, already has everything, which is also true. In that paradox of perspective is one of the secrets to retention.

What difference does perspective make? Simply this: Each day—either consciously or unconsciously—every employee in your corporation chooses a philosophy of ministry which will be the organizing principle for their choices, values, ethical concerns, and business practices. Their philosophy of ministry might be linked to their religious beliefs, or the lack of them; it could be linked to a certain set of family or cultural values, or it could be linked to the last television show they watched. Whatever influences they choose, the choice will be a spiritual one, because it reflects one's values, character, morality, and desires. As an employer responsible for the majority of your employee's productive waking hours, wouldn't you like to positively influence the crafting of these "soft" but very influential elements? Do you think these choices impact your employees' productivity and, ultimately, your company's profitability? Absolutely they do.

The crafting of individual and corporate philosophies of ministry in the workplace brings multiple pay-offs. It confronts people with the impact of their personal choices, teaches them to live in the present, to appreciate what they have now, and to actively seek out the joy and hope in what is, not what someday might be. Along these lines, the Dalai Lama inquires, rhetorically,

> "How do we place our cushions? How do we brush our teeth? How do we sweep our floor, or slice a carrot? We think we are here to deal with more important issues, such as our problems with our partner, our jobs, our health, and the like. We don't want to bother with the little things, like how we hold our chopsticks, or where we place our spoon. Yet these acts are the stuff of our life, moment to moment. It's not a question of importance, it's a question of paying attention, being aware. Why? Because each moment in life is absolute in itself. That's all there is."

In other words, we all have a philosophy of ministry whether it is articulated or not; so let's take the logical step and bring our philosophy of ministry to a conscious level. The implications of an articulated philosophy of ministry, and the learned art of appreciating the present, are immeasurable, both for individual and corporate performance, and for qualitative and quantitative growth.

Immeasurable because they have to do with character, which has to do with trust, which is a soft commodity that both clients and the best employees value immensely.

TAKE YOUR OWN SPIRITUAL INVENTORY

Once you understand *why* a philosophy of ministry is important, the next step is to take your own spiritual inventory. Employers need to model at the leadership level those qualities they want their employees to live out. Of course, no one is a perfect model of anything, and everyone, even those with the best intentions, experience failure from time to time. On the other hand, no one appreciates a hypocrite. Employees want to see leaders exemplifying a chosen philosophy of ministry. All employees desire a certain amount of mentoring from their leaders. This explains why any discussion of spirituality in the workplace must begin with you, the leader. We all hold spiritual values whether we acknowledge them or not, the purpose of this step is to bring these beliefs to a conscious level. Thus, we begin by asking what spiritual values do you hold? What do you believe about "transcendent reality" (i.e., God, or a higher power)? How are these intangibles valued in your life? How are they evident? More specifically, how does the way you organize your life around those intangibles translate to the way you treat and value your employees?

Your answers to these questions are the building blocks for developing an effective philosophy of ministry, one that will attract and keep the best employees. Perhaps the most important spiritual question for every leader to answer in advance is, "What are the most important personal values and beliefs I bring to my work?" Trust? Honesty? Vulnerability? Open-mindedness? Candor? Compassion? Patience? Perseverance? Following personal passion in one's work? Being part of a team that works well together? Making unique and creative contributions? Trouble-shooting and problem-solving? Whatever you value, it is vital to identify them.

Left unidentified they can easily be usurped by more trivial issues and consumed by the day-to-day activities of surviving in business.

But perhaps you think more simply about these things. For you, generating profits for the company is the most important consideration, regardless of how that happens. After all, without a profit there's no purpose in talking about spirituality at all, right? If you believe that, you are not alone, having chosen a widely accepted ethical position shared by many in business. (By the way, this position has a twin brother with whom you are no doubt also familiar: "The end justifies the means.")

"Process, shmocess," you say, "just get the work out, period." However, this ethical barometer renders any discussion of spirituality moot, because spirituality is all about process and what happens along the way, and what happens to people in that process. If the end does justify the means people become expendable commodities, reduced to servicing the profit margin, period. But if you are interested in both profits and people (not, as some say, profits through people) spirituality has a place in your organization and can actually become a profit center. Your company spends significant capital to recruit, train and support your best talent. Keeping them costs less than losing them, and employees remain where they feel they are valued as persons. So, I would again remind you: the "process" of integrating a healthy spirituality into your business begins with you and other leaders identifying your values, with identifying those beliefs you see as most important, both personally and professionally.

To illustrate this, let's review the lessons of a frequently used time management exercise that I recently witnessed. The exercise was conducted by an expert in time management who was speaking to a group of business students. As he stood in front of the group of high-powered over-achievers he said, "Okay, time for a quiz." He pulled out a one-gallon, wide mouth Mason jar and set it on the table in front of him. Next he produced about a dozen fist-sized rocks and carefully placed them, one at a time, into the jar. When the jar was filled to the top and no more rocks would fit inside, he asked, "Is this jar full?" Everyone in the class said, "Yes." Then he said, "Really?"

He reached under the table and pulled out a bucket of gravel. Then he dumped some gravel in and shook the jar causing pieces of gravel to work themselves down into the space between the big rocks. Then he asked the group once more, "Is the jar full?" By this time the class was on to him. "Probably not," one of them answered. "Good!" he replied. He reached under the table and brought out a bucket of sand. He started dumping the sand in the jar and it went into all of the spaces left between the rocks and the gravel.

Once more he asked the question, "Is this jar full?" "No!" the class shouted. Once again he said, "Good." Then he grabbed a pitcher of water and began to pour it in until the jar was filled to the brim. Then he looked at the class and asked, "What is the point of this illustration?"

One eager beaver raised his hand and said, "The point is, no matter how full your schedule is, if you try really hard you can always fit some more things into it!" "No," the speaker replied, "not the point at all. The illustration teaches this truth: *If you don't put the big rocks in first, you'll never get them in at all.*"

AND THE POINT IS . . . ?: What are the building blocks, the "big rocks" in your personal life? Your children? Your loved ones? Your education? Your dreams? A worthy cause? Teaching or mentoring others? Doing things that you love? Time for yourself? Your health? Your significant other? And what are the "big rocks" in your business life—those intangible values you deem most important (e.g., trust, honesty, open-mindedness, candor, compassion, patience, perseverance)? Putting the big rocks in first means you're sure to get them in. Sweating the little stuff (the gravel, the sand) will fill your life with things that don't really matter. To have the quality time you need to spend on the big, important stuff (the big rocks), first identify them, and then organize your life around them.

IN ORDER TO DO THIS, right now, before you forget or have an excuse (a small rock or piece of pea gravel) take a moment to reflect on the story and ask yourself: what are the "big rocks" in your personal life, and how, specifically, will you begin organizing your life so they have first place in the jar? Second, what are the "big rocks" in your professional life, those intangibles you value most and around which you can begin to organize your life so they have first place in the jar? To answer these, you first have to know what the big rocks are. So take a quick little "spiritual inventory." Defining one's priorities is a spiritual task because it taps into our concerns about our own mortality, what life will be like at the end, once we're gone. What must you accomplish by the end of your life—occupationally, personally, relationally—in order to have a sense of contentment and satisfaction? Right now, what remains left undone in your life, which must be put in the jar first? What legacy do you want to leave your family, your children, business associates, and friends? What can you do to make sure these get done, and "on time," so to speak? Once defined, the next step is to arrange your life to accommodate the new shift in priorities. This means you will probably need to say "no" to some things that seem important now, and "yes" to some things that have value for the future. What are some things you will need to say "no" to now? Spirituality focuses both on teaching us to be able to enjoy the present moments of our lives with grace and contentment, while holding ever before us our own mortality. Author Joan McIntosh wrote, "Accept the pain, cherish the joys, resolve the regrets; then can come the best of benedictions—'If I had my life to live over, I'd do it all the same.'"

LESSONS FROM THE RICHEST MAN
WHO EVER LIVED

There are many lessons that we can learn about the importance of values and a philosophy of ministry from King Solomon. King Solomon lived around 900 B.C.E. and was the son of the great Israelite King David and his wife Bathsheba. Solomon reigned during the years when Israel reached its greatest prosperity and glory. In the fourth year of Solomon's reign, about 966 B.C.E. he began the construction of his famous temple, which lasted seven or eight years and which, in today's dollars would have cost about $10 billion to complete (10 Billion!). According to Old Testament tradition, on the day the temple was dedicated even God showed up for the festivities (see 1 Kings 8). Solomon composed remarkable works on natural history and practical philosophy, and wrote beautiful poetic verse (see the Song of Solomon). Much of the book of Proverbs is attributed to him as well.

For all his talent and wealth, it was his success and prosperity that eventually led to his undoing, and his unlimited power led to unlimited arrogance and self-indulgence. After a few decades Israel's prosperity dwindled and economic hardship became widespread, leading to a popular revolt. Solomon's last years were embittered by personal disillusionment and by hostility at home and abroad. When Solomon died, his incompetent son, Rehoboam, could not hold the Hebrew empire together and the kingdom split in two.

Solomon was brilliant, handsome, had it all and did it all. And in his Old Testament opus known as *"The Book of Ecclesiastes"* he wrote honestly about the glories of his lifestyle, as well as its drawbacks. The book is worth a read, regardless of whether you are of the Judeo-Christian persuasion, because Solomon's wisdom comes from direct experience of having had everything most people want, and having achieved everything most only dream of. Like most leaders, Solomon was a manager, a visionary, a delegator, and a builder. And he built his empire on a philosophy of ministry, of service that acknowledged the importance of the transcendent or the divine.

He wrote Ecclesiastes toward the end of his career, as a kind of advice column, warning how to avoid falling into the same patterns and delusions which had spelled his ruin. The message of the book can be stated in three propositions. First, when one looks at life with its seemingly aimless cycles (1:4ff.) and inexplicable paradoxes (4:1; 7:15; 8:8), one might conclude that all of living is futile, since it is impossible to discern any purpose in the ordering of events. Second, nevertheless, life is to be enjoyed to the fullest, realizing that it is a gift of God (3:12-13; 3:22; 5:18-19; 8:15; 9:7-9). And third, the wise person will live their life in close relationship to the Divine (3:16-17; 12:14).

Note the following testimony from the wisest and wealthiest man who ever lived: "I denied myself nothing my eyes desired; I refused my heart no pleasure. Yet . . . everything was meaningless, a chasing after the wind" (2:10-11). "God gives a man wealth, possessions and honor, so that he lacks nothing his heart desires; but God does not enable him to enjoy them" (6:2). "All man's efforts are for his mouth, yet his appetite is never satisfied" (6:7).

The theme Solomon re-directs our attention to is that wanting, getting and having it all may bring many things, but it doesn't bring deep contentment or personal satisfaction. Never has, never will. Yet the religion of many in Western culture is the religion of accumulation, whether of wealth, possessions, people, or power. And exactly what might this have to do with retaining employees? Precisely this: the leader who worships only at the altar of accumulation will attract talent who also desire to worship only those same gods. They will work for that leader as long as they are able to accumulate whatever it is that drives them. That leader will attract persons who don't necessarily love the work, or want to be part of a team, or want to deliver good product or service. They will work for the boss because the boss is accumulating, and because they believe they can accumulate too. Of course, the trouble with this kind of leadership and its motivation is that when tough times hit, as they always do, employees leave for greener pastures. Employees whose only motivation is accumulation will leave when the potential is no longer there. Thus, a business's ability to accumulate wealth and power may be important for a variety of other reasons, but it is seldom a good employee retention strategy. Solomon's kingdom and his leadership split up over the unchecked motivation for "more."

AND THE POINT IS . . . ?: If you want to retain talent who are in it for more than the money, you must be in it for more than the money, and learn effective ways to communicate and model alternative motivations.

HOW?: Having now identified your values and beliefs, practice living from them. Let your employees know about them (without at the same time heralding your great virtue from the mountaintops). Don't plan on living them perfectly. Leave yourself and your employees plenty of room for failure. Value individual motives. And remember Solomon's advice: Enjoy life for the divine gift it is (2:24), make the most of every opportunity (9:10), and live life with a respect for that which is spiritual (12:13). And I would add, never, ever take yourself too seriously.

PART 2: UNDERSTAND THE TWO SPIRITUAL NEEDS THAT ALL EMPLOYEES SHARE

The World Future Society recently named the top ten new products that will change the way we work and live over the next decade. Among them were multi-fuel automobiles running on combinations of electricity, reformulated gasoline, natural gas, and other fuels, home health monitors which give automatic analysis of one's vital signs, and smart maps and tracking devices, good for finding a

Chinese restaurant or a lost dog. Each reflects a growing emphasis on global and personal efficiency, and on the value of time.

Additionally, The Brand Futures Group recently identified ten shift-shapers that will define the next decade. These include what they term "Generation Blur," referencing new work and lifestyles for thirty-and forty-somethings, wherein life-stage, not demographics, will be the most important criterion for market segmentation. They predict an evolution in business perception from green to blue, suggesting that companies must be seen as doing good, not just doing no harm. They project increasing need for security and privacy where the home is seen as a fortress against Big Brother (referencing an American Management Association survey, which indicates that two-thirds of employers eavesdrop on employees via phone, e-mail, or the internet). They predict the development of "No-brow" culture, citing that the rise of discount retailers has prompted the rise of the anti-status customer. They predict that personal R&R will be big business, noting that in 1998, $2 billion in candles and accessories were sold and that aromatherapy products will continue to sell as coping strategies for stress. And they look for "The Big Shrink," as the culture continues to move toward a decline in the "more is more" mindset (*Training and Development*, April 2000).

These predictions reflect a complex market, a market interested in both personal and corporate ethics, and in protecting personal privacy. They mirror a society increasingly less enamored with status and more interested in economy of effort and resources. They tell of a culture "working hard to avoid stress," and seeking personal peace by way of simplification.

Ethics. Privacy. Peace. Simplificaton. Spiritual issues, all. They are spiritual because they connect to one's hunger for qualities that are transcendent, beyond the physical or material. These hungers are basic to what it means to be human. By extension then, not only is it vital for business to pay attention to them in the global marketplace, it is just as vital for individual businesses to pay attention to them as they manifest themselves in the employees down the hall.

While corporate environments are always changing, people's basic needs remain the same. If you know what they are you can build a sensitivity to them into your philosophy of ministry. Two basic needs that all people desire to have met through work are Hospitality and Meaning. We'll look at each to see how they can be implemented in the work environment in ways that communicate to the employee that he or she is a valuable asset, valued not only for their performance but for who they are as persons.

AND THE POINT IS . . . ?: Employees voluntarily leave companies for two non-remunerative reasons: (a) they leave when they feel they are not valued for their performance, and/or (b) when they are not valued for who they are as individuals. By paying specific attention to the basic human need to be valued, employees will sense they are appreciated for who they are as persons, not just as performers.

HOW? First, introduce the language of valuing others. Reference the language in inter-office memos, staff meetings, and in informal conversation. Second, be "hospitable." This communicates an employer's interest in the personal bottom-line, not just the corporate one. This pays off in employee loyalty.

HOSPITALITY

How do you show that a company is "hospitable?" First, understand that employees want to be made to feel "at home" in a company. This doesn't mean a leader's job is to make them feel comfortable all the time, or to cater to their every whim. No, employees simply want to know that their company, and particularly their immediate leadership are hospitable toward them. To illustrate the idea of hospitality, take an example from your own household. When you walk through your door at the end of a long day, you may enjoy being met by someone or something that breathes (for most, this reduces your options to a person or a pet; and a person, whom you like, is probably a good first option). You want attention. Maybe some small acknowledgement that you have arrived, and survived. You want to feel you are in an environment where you are relatively safe, where there is an attitude of relaxed appreciation for who you are, and where there are rules against abuse, either explicit or implied. You also want a Swedish massage, a chilled beverage and a gourmet dinner—but you can't have everything. And neither can your employees. But they can expect a basic level of hospitality from their work environment and as leader you can set the tone.

HOW? Two ways a leader can be hospitable include attentive listening and encouraging a pace at work that reflects your conviction that they are, indeed, human and not divine.

FIRST: LISTEN WELL

Listening is an art whose medium is time. Think about this for a moment. Listening takes time. Because listening takes time, if good listening were a marketable commodity the demand would drastically exceed the supply. It takes valuable time to listen to another, to truly hear what is being said beyond the words, to the intentions of the heart, to one's motives or hopes. Listening is a simple gift that you can give your employees which costs you little (though I acknowledge, time is money), and which communicates a sense of hospitality every time. Perhaps more than anything a leader can do, listening intently to the needs, complaints, concerns, ideas or celebrations of an employee is the greatest example of hospitality, or, literally, of "hosting" another.

In his offering titled *Threads*, James A. Autry paints a sensitive portrayal of the value of listening beyond the spoken words:

> *Sometimes you just connect*
> *like that,*
> *no big thing maybe*
> *but something beyond the usual business stuff.*
> *It comes and goes quickly*
> *so you have to pay attention,*
> *a change in the eyes*
> *when you ask about the family,*
> *a pain flickering behind the statistics*
> *about a boy and a girl in school,*
> *or about seeing them every other Sunday.*
> *An older guy talks about his bride,*
> *a little affectation after twenty-five years.*
> *A hot-eyed achiever laughs before you want him to.*
> *Someone tells about his wife's job*
> *or why she quit working to stay home.*
> *An old joker needs another laugh on the way*
> *to retirement.*
> *A woman says she spends a lot of her salary*
> *on an au pair*
> *and a good one is hard to find*
> *but worth it because there's nothing more important*
> *than the baby.*
> *Listen.*
> *In every office*
> *you hear the threads*
> *of love and joy and fear and guilt,*
> *the cries for celebration and reassurance,*
> *and somehow you know that connecting those threads*
> *is what you are supposed to do*
> *and business takes care of itself.*

SECOND: SLOW DOWN

Mary Wilson Little wrote, "There is no pleasure in having nothing to do; the fun is in having lots to do and not doing it." While this may be a psychological truth, it's not something you want to put up on posters around the office. So, what I'm about to say goes primarily for the personality type known affectionately as the workaholic. And, if you're honest, those are the ones you particularly want to keep, but they're also the ones you want to keep from burning out. For these high-powered, self-motivated, over-achievers we prescribe a seemingly antithetical suggestion: slow down. That's right, slow down. Slow the work pace. Take a day off. Or two. Or three. Relax (Warning: this hasn't been known to be an effective hospitality strategy with those affectionately known as slugs, but then you aren't trying to retain them anyway).

Especially at times when things around the shop have been at a fever pitch, by giving your best employees permission to slow down you demonstrate your trust in their ability to continue to perform at optimum levels while at once communicating your concern for their personal well-being. In fact, by encouraging them to moderate their pace a bit, you may find that you actually encourage a fresh form of creative energy to emerge. The great American conductor and composer Leonard Bernstein wrote:

> *"Still is our most intense mode of action. It is in our moments of deep quiet that is born every idea, emotion, and drive which we eventually honor with the name of action. Our most emotionally active life is lived in our dreams, and our cells renew themselves most industriously in sleep. We reach highest in meditation, and farthest in prayer. In stillness every human being is great; he is free from the experience of hostility; he is a poet, and most like an angel."*

The shadow side of expressing ourselves through our labors is the possibility of workaholism, perfectionism, and excessive busyness. The Chinese word for "busy" is composed of two characters: "heart" and "killing." When we busy ourselves to the point that we are always rushing around trying to get this or that "done," or "over with," we kill something vital in ourselves. When excessive judgment and impatience characterize our work, or if we are constantly striving for speed and efficiency, we lose our own sense of hospitality. Put another way, we lose our *selves* in the work, and not in a positive way. Whatever we may be seeking through our frantic productivity and accomplishments (be it approval, distraction, filling the spiritual void, competitive advantage, etc.) we lose a sense of who we truly are, and what our real desires are. In frenetic, anxious activity—however productive it may be—we are not being hospitable to ourselves.

Pulling down a bit of Solomonic wisdom from *Ecclesiastes*, one proverb reads, "Better one hand full of quiet than two hands full of striving after wind." Unpracticed in the art of a balanced work pace, we hope to find our sense of hospitality, our belonging, and even perhaps our healing by increasing our levels of accomplishment. But our frenetic busyness actually makes us deaf to what is productive and whole, both in ourselves and in those with whom we work.[2]

MEANING

Employees are more likely to stay with employers who understand their basic spiritual needs. We've seen that a first need, that of experiencing a basic sense of hospitality, can be expressed by an

---

[2] For an understanding of the high price that people, organizations, societies and cultures are paying to live at warp speed, read *Hyperculture: The Human Cost Of Speed* (By Stephen Bertman, published by Praeger). Bertman describes the "power of now" and its impact on the family, society, the environment and democracy.

employer via the art of attentive listening, and by giving top performers permission to slow the pace at times. In so doing, leaders communicate their interest in employees as persons.

A second spiritual need, shared by a majority of employees, is finding a sense of meaning and purpose in their work. Rabbi Harold Kushner wrote,

> *"Most of us don't fear death as much as we fear coming to the end of our lives and realizing that we never lived."*

Since employees spend the majority of their waking hours working, they naturally draw a great sense of personal meaning from the events and interactions they experience in the workplace. They want to know that they aren't just working, they are "living." The search for, and lack of personal meaning in a confusing and conflicted world is epidemic and thwarts the sense that one is living in meaningful ways. How does one go about finding meaning for one's life? According to Victor Frankl, holocaust survivor and psychologist,

> *"Meanings are inexhaustible. We need to develop our intuitive sense that allows us to smell out meanings hidden and dormant in life situations."*

Meaning is inherent in many situations and circumstances. The issue seems to be whether we are open to finding it, and then knowing it when we see it.

With that as a foundation, here are several practical things a leader can do to help employees draw a sense of meaning from their daily work lives:

SOMETIMES THE HARDEST THING TO DO IS TO SIMPLY LOOK FOR IT. The biggest challenge in finding meaning in one's day-to-day work activities is deciphering the lessons in the simplest of encounters—hallway conversations, an article read over lunch, a quote on the wall of a co-worker's office, the criticism of a peer, or the private moments immediately preceding an important meeting—in each of these we can train ourselves to ask, "What does this mean?", "What meaning does this impart to my life or to my work?", "Why does this matter?" Often, we aren't looking for meaning in the mundane or the ordinary, and so we don't find it. A manager might consider convening a discussion, either informally, over lunch, or formally, as part of a regularly scheduled meeting, to discuss how, and if employees currently find meaning in their work, and what differences it makes in their work product when they do find work meaningful.

LOOK FOR MEANING IN THE WRITTEN WORD. Via e-mail or fax, an employer can send regular quotes, or thoughts which express how he or she finds meaning in their work. Print media has a way of getting around. The messages you communicate by the quotes you choose reveal a great deal about your business philosophy and your core values, both as employer and as fellow human being. An interesting (and literal) illustration of the power of words to influence is offered by Rabbi David Wolpe who writes that,

> *"In many traditional Jewish communities, when a child entered cheder—religious school—for the first time, that child was greeted by a curious sight: a chart of letters smeared with honey. The new student licked off the honey from the letters one by one, thus learning a critical lesson: learning is sweet, and the very letters of the word carry the sweetness."*

LOOK FOR MEANING IN LIFE'S FINITENESS. Life is short, and the older we get the truer it seems. Employers do their employees a great service if they can determine effective ways to keep "the big picture" before employees; that is, that today's challenges are part of the tapestry of our lives. Today's challenges are not our life. Note the difference, it's a small shift in language, but if you get it, it can save you thousands in therapy bills! As difficult as the challenges are today, today is only one day. And in the grand scope of one's entire life, today's struggles and disappointments are relatively small. It's a matter of perspective, and as a leader and influencer of people, you can communicate a fresh perspective in ways that take the edge off the anxiety produced by those daily struggles. For example, find some stories about getting perspective that have meaning for you personally. Put them on your wall. Send them in an e-mail when an employee is feeling overwhelmed. If you're a story-teller by nature, memorize some stories and verbally share them with employees at appropriate times. For example, inspirational writer Robert Fulghum relays the following story, illustrating how to find meaning by taking a few minutes for a personal retrospective:

> *A caption for this photograph: A man sitting on a folding chair in a cemetery, as a light rain fell and the sun shone at the same time, on the first day of summer in 1994. If you were there, standing close by, you would notice that the sod beneath his chair was laid down in small square sections, suggesting it had been removed and then carefully replaced. The man owns the property upon which he sits. He has paid for the site, paid to have the ground dug up, to have a cement vault installed, and to have the ground restored. He is sitting on his own grave. Not because his death is imminent—he's in pretty good shape, actually. And not because he was in a morbid*

state of mind—he was in a fine mood when the pic-
ture was taken. In fact, while sitting there on his
own grave, he has had one of the most affirmative
afternoons of his life. Sitting for an afternoon on his
own grave, he has had one of those potent experi-
ences when the large pattern of one's life is unex-
pectedly reviewed: the past, birth, childhood, ado-
lescence, marriage, career, the present, and the
future. He has confronted finitude—the limits of
life. The fact of his own death lies before him and
beneath him—raising the questions of the when and
the where and the how of it. What shall he do with
his life between now and then?

As an employer you can help employees develop and maintain healthy perspectives of their work by juxtaposing how hard the challenges seem now, with how bad it could be. In a humorous way, Margaret Stevens gives an example of a story that teaches just that:

[There was] a man who died and found himself in a
beautiful place, surrounded by every conceivable
comfort. A white jacketed man came to him and
said, "You may have anything you choose—any
food—any pleasure—any kind of entertainment."
The man was delighted, and for days he sampled all
the delicacies and experiences of which he had
dreamed on earth. But one day he grew bored with
all of it, and calling the attendant to him, he said,
"I'm tired of all this. I need something to do. What
kind of work can you give me?" The attendant sadly
shook his head and replied, "I'm sorry, sir. That's the
one thing we can't do for you. There is no work here
for you." To which the man answered, "That's a fine

thing. I might as well be in hell." The attendant said softly, "Where do you think you are?"

EXERCISE: Have employees write their epitaphs as a way of envisioning what the final product of their lives might look like. Then have them relate it to their work by asking them to write an ideal epitaph of what their area or department will look like when they retire, or move on. When it's all over, what would they like said about their lives and their legacies at work? What would you, as their leader, like said—and not said?! A little morbid, perhaps, but effective, because it makes the point that as a leader, you are concerned about how your employees' work life fits the context of their entire life. The poet May Sarton wrote this eulogy to a friend:

Death Frames the essential. What was framed for us on that final day is hard to put into words, elusive. Perhaps what we mourned was a whole man. All the fragments of a life that had sometimes seemed to scatter itself among too many gifts came together, and we saw him whole. And we began to see what the wholeness was all about—a capacity for pure joy, a capacity for tenderness rarely seen in a man. It was the human triumph of one who had . . . never ceased to create and to give.

It is good for a professional to be reminded that his professionalism is only a husk, that the real person must remain an amateur, a lover of the work. Whatever we do well is done spontaneously for its own sake. . . . I am, I think, more of a poet than I was before I knew him, if to be a poet means allowing life to flow through one, rather than forcing it to a mold the will has shaped; if it means learning to let the day shape the work, not the work, the day, and so live toward essence as naturally as a bird or a flower.

CONCLUSION

Upon review, this chapter really has very little to do with spirituality per se. In contemporary culture spirituality seems to serve as the latest synonym for personal happiness, as if to say, "If it makes me happy, it must be spiritual." This chapter also has little to do with employers keeping employees happy on the job, though that may be a result. The Chapter has, I think, more to do with contentment. We think we want happiness, or joy but when we say those things I think what we really want is to be content, that is, to be able to be happy and joyful in any situation, regardless of circumstances, regardless of what (or who) we have or don't have, regardless of whether we had a successful quarter or a miserable one. Contentment. We want it, need it, desire it, pursue it, pay money for it, sacrifice our bodies, and give up relationships for it. We devote extreme amounts of attention to get it, sacrifice our children for it, leave locations to find it, change jobs in pursuit of it. Depending on which author, televangelist, or motivational speaker we happen to run across on a given day, we can easily be talked in to believing that contentment can be "gotten," "achieved," "harnessed," "found," or "bought."

Do a quick little mental review: Is it not true that, for the most part, the moments of contentment you enjoy most take you by surprise? It is not that we seize them, but that they seize us? We have a tendency to convince ourselves that life will be better after we get married, or have a baby, buy a house, or change neighborhoods. We tell ourselves that life will be complete when our boss, our spouse or significant other gets his or her act together. Or when we get a nicer car, or are able to take a vacation, or when we switch departments, or when we retire. However, there's no better time to be open to contentment seizing us than right now, in these present circumstances. For if not now, when? Life will always be filled with challenges. It's best simply to admit that and decide to be open to contentment seizing us along the way, even in the midst of the struggles.

Writer Alfred D. Souza said, "For a long time it had seemed to me that life was about to begin—real life. But there was always some obstacle in the way, something to be gotten through first, some unfinished business, time still to be served, and a debt to be paid. Then life would begin. At last it dawned on me that these obstacles were my life." Souza's perspective helps us see that there is indeed no specific method, equation, key or secret to contentment. Contentment is present in what you're doing right now. The question is not a question of "how" but of "whether": whether we will choose to see in the present moment the seeds of contentment and joy living there already, waiting for us to choose to live in and through them. To decide that there is no better time than right now is to know contentment. It is the journey, not a destination. It's the road you're on, not the place you arrive.

So what? Well, we certainly can do things to encourage our experience of contentment. As leaders of people we can work to increase the possibility of contentment among our employees by modeling hospitable behaviors and developing an atmosphere where employees find meaning and a sense of connectedness to something bigger than themselves. But it is very difficult to manufacture, measure or judge the presence or the impact of spirituality or the quality of contentment that proceeds from it. Though, as we've said, just because something doesn't fit in a test tube doesn't mean it's not real. As a matter of fact it may just be bottom-line spiritual.

REFERENCES

*Autry, James A.. **Love and Profit**.*

*Bernstein, Leonard (1976). **Findings**.*

*Fulghum, Robert. From **Beginning to End**.*

*Sarton, May. **Plant Dreaming Deep**.*

FROM DICTATOR TO FACILITATOR

*Retaining Employees Using
the ACTOR Strategy*

By Ed Rose

OVERVIEW

*This chapter illustrates the importance of developing five
Leadership qualities that support a culture of participative
management and pro-active retention within an organization.
Ed Rose has been there in the trenches and he has learned how
to increase retention through effective person-to-person management. This chapter focuses on Ed Rose's personal transition
from Dictator to Facilitator. Ed shares with you the five
Leadership qualities that he believes have helped him and his
organization move from a sweatshop to a team-based organization benchmarked by over 100 companies from around
the world! Ed's company, Intersil Corporation, received the*

prestigious Leadership for Excellence Award from the Work in America Institute in 1999.

INTRODUCTION

For sixteen years, Ed Rose was a traditional, command-and-control production manager and he was good at it. Then the company wanted him to become a coach and then train others. Guess what ... he became good at it.

IN THE BEGINNING—THE DICTATOR

In the beginning I had just been laid off from Kennedy Space Center and was looking for a job. In November 1972, I decided to accept a position with a new semiconductor company as a manufacturing supervisor. It seemed exciting. All I had to do was to set a monthly goal and go for it. Fast pace, daily fire fighting, and never a dull moment. To me the job was just like playing sports ... winning was making the schedule, trying to be the best in the department, finding the fastest and best solution to problems, and getting recognized for your efforts. Guess what I discovered in the traditional management culture ... if you stand out enough and if you meet schedules no matter what, you'll get promoted.

By 1975 I truly believed I had found my calling. I was working in an environment that wanted me to use the skills I had learned in military school. All I had to do was to keep the troops (employees) in line. If the employees needed an opinion, I gave them one (and I did just that often). In fact, I was so good at it my bosses loved it. I was doing just what they expected of me. I even learned new ways to "motivate" employees. I called it management by electrocution: "I'm not sure what's going to happen to you, but you can be sure if you don't do what I've directed you to do, something bad is going to happen." Oh, yes, let's not leave out management's need to establish an adversarial relationship between manufacturing and engineering. It seemed this type of conflict was viewed as a positive force in our organizational culture. I was in my element, the toughest guy on the floor.

By 1978, I had developed into a respected (feared) production supervisor. I had complete control in the production area and the engineers would avoid any interaction with me. Management rewarded me for my obvious ability to motivate people and take charge by promoting me to production manager. I had arrived. I was happy! Or was I? The job got really tough. As Harry Truman said, "the buck stops here." Well, I felt like the whole company's success depended on my ability to meet schedules. All the "bucks" seemed to stop at my door.

By 1980, the workload had increased to a point where the job took all my focus, with little time for extracurricular activities or my children. Every extra minute was devoted to my job. After all, without me it would fail! Right? I had to "motivate" everyone to meet their schedules! Right!

By 1988, now 10 years as a production manager, I had the reputation of being one of the biggest "kick butt, take names" production managers in the company.

GROW OR GO

Then, suddenly, with the company growing, several forward-looking managers were promoted to leadership positions and they envisioned a company with an empowered workforce. Change was in the air. At this point, my reputation began working against me. Management wanted a change, and guess what ... it was me!

They gave me an ultimatum. It can be summed up in these words ... grow or go. Some of my first thoughts were — I've devoted my life to this company, this can't be happening! I started to think of all the schedules I had made and the revenue that I brought into the company. My life, to this point, had been pretty standard, just like military school, very much a routine. It was about to change and I didn't know what to expect. Consequently, my sense of security was threatened, but I decided that growing was better than going, so I took the plunge.

As I look back, my boss had incredible wisdom. He understood the conflict between balancing the organization's need for change with the need for me to maintain a certain sense of security. He moved slowly, respecting my need for security and maintaining my self-esteem.

Upon removing me from my position, my boss offered me a choice of jobs. I chose to be a JIT (Just-In-Time) facilitator, a job focused on coaching employees in their selected improvement projects. During this period I was fortunate to have a mentor, Dr. Louis Martin-Vega, a professor who was doing some consulting work for the company. I studied under him and eventually took his program throughout the company. I attribute my understanding about change, as well as my present teaching skills, to Dr. Martin-Vega.

Coaching was always a strong point of mine during the time that I was managing my electrocution at work. I was coaching young boys in the games of football, baseball and basketball, and also coaching grown men in softball. Interestingly I had seldom used these skills in my work environment because only results, bottom line dollars, was rewarded. In this new culture, however, senior leadership encouraged these skills and sent me to training classes to enhance them.

By 1989, in an extraordinary, 180° turn of events, the former "electrocutioner", the former "baddest dude on the block," was traveling to other plants conducting training sessions for JIT and coaching employees at different sites. This was a new experience for me and very interesting. By now, of course, my boss didn't think I had enough to do; so he assigned me to the training department with a focus on facilitating the implementation of self-directed work teams (SDWTs) within my old department.

I put the same energy into this new assignment as I had my previous jobs. I contributed greatly to the implementation of SDWTs, working closely with the internal consultant. I even created new tools used in the implementation process.

By 1991, my boss was now a plant manager and wanted to start SDWTs in the entire division. He asked me to help accomplish this by serving as the training manager of the division. Working with some close associates within the company, we put together a structured approach to developing a team-based environment. This process has since been benchmarked by several companies in the U.S. as well as some in Ireland, Spain and Australia.

By 1993, only five years removed from the old "kick butt, take names" person I used to be, I was presenting on how to be an effective coach at various national conferences. Companies were asking me to talk about how I had made the transition from "Dictator to Facilitator." Additionally, companies from around the world were benchmarking Intersil (still called Harris Semiconductor at this point). We were so successful that we had to limit the companies who wanted to visit our site because it was distracting from our production. Our employees were role models for team involvement. Employees enjoyed their work instead of looking forward to quitting time. They were being trained on the job in conflict management and various other interpersonal skills. This was a new company and a new Ed Rose.

LESSONS FROM MY JOURNEY FROM DICTATOR TO FACILITATOR

I am sure my story is not unique and I am sure most readers can relate to it either personally or because they know someone like Ed Rose. At least this has been the feedback from the numerous presentations I have made around the world on this subject. The story is meant to give the readers a foundation for the transformation both personally and organizationally. The reason the transformation is critical for retention should be obvious. Who wants to work for a company with the mentality of management by electrocution? Not many ... I didn't even want to. If we had lived in Silicon Valley I likely would not have lasted two years. The importance of this chapter is the lessons both the organization and Ed Rose learned during the transition.

I looked back and asked myself, why did it take the organization, why did it take me, so long to get here?

Let's talk about leadership for minute:

My management style served me well for a good part of my life, and it wasn't until the culture started to change at Harris, and elsewhere around the United States, that I became aware that it might not be the most effective leadership style. Today, textbooks and authors often refer to this style as the "traditional leader." But was it the most effective? It definitely can be effective, but it only works in the short term. Was this the only paradigm available for leaders to learn from? No! History shows that there have been other successful approaches to leadership.

A 17th century Russian field marshal, Count Suvorov, never lost a battle, not even against numerically superior opponents. Suvorov had a "secret weapon." He recognized that the enlisted soldier was the *foundation* of his success. He trained and encouraged his front line soldiers to be their best. He treated them with *respect*. There were other leaders who also shared this "secret weapon." Attila the Hun, Sitting Bull and many others who trained and encouraged their people in their own way during the times they lived. In fact, even some of the ancient Greek warriors understood this to be the best way to lead. So why didn't we learn from history?

To learn effectively whether from the past or present we must have "paradigm flexibility." We have to remain adaptable and not get ourselves locked into having only one way to do something. The opposite of paradigm flexibility is "paradigm paralysis," where you have only one fixed thought or context to operate from. Simply said, a leader must be adaptable. I believe that both history and my experience has proven that leadership is about being trustworthy, which is essential for earning the commitment and respect of your followers.

Committed people follow their leaders. Leaders such as Suvorov, Sitting Bull and Pericles learned the importance of their *followers* being resourceful, and they recognized the need to provide training in the areas that would help them make better decisions and be more effective in action. They also realized the need for their followers to maintain an optimistic outlook, which required the leader to establish a positive vision of the future, for them, their families, and their people. Finally, through their actions, these leaders demonstrated consideration for their followers by being committed to excellence. When employees have a commitment to their leader this translates into a positive retention tool. Creating a culture of this type generates word-of-mouth advertising that no company can buy.

SUMMARY

Today you can't pick up a business magazine and not find at least one example of these effective leadership behaviors. But it seems that many, perhaps most, organizations still haven't embraced what it takes to have every leader become an effective one. Here are the five Qualities that I call "ACTOR," summarizing what I've learned from my transition from Dictator to Facilitator. I believe these leadership qualities are timeless.

FIVE EFFECTIVE LEADERSHIP QUALITIES FOR RETENTION (ACTOR)

ADAPTABLE

Leaders must be adaptable to change. Charles Darwin said, "It's not the strongest of the species, nor the most intelligent, that survive; it's the one most responsive to change." Your job as a leader is to allow change to occur and, in some cases, to be the catalyst. The last thing you want is to be the keeper of the tradition that creates the roadblock to progress. Learn to challenge both the process and your current thinking. Have "paradigm flexibility."

Look for creative ways to solve problems. I have heard it said that Death is life's way of saying "IT'S TIME FOR A CHANGE." In the business world death comes to both employees and organizations who don't recognize the signs of change and act to minimize its effect. Developing the leadership quality of being adaptable helps you and the organization recognize the need for change before it's too late for you and/or the organization. Being adaptable should be a core competency in organizations that expect to flourish in the new millennium.

CONSIDERATION

As the leader, you must consider your role carefully, but you can no longer think in terms of "the end justifies the means." You must consider the personal effect of your actions on your followers if you are to build the commitment that's required for long-term success. Leaders don't use their position to gain special perks. What's good enough for your followers should be good enough for you. Leaders should also look to celebrate the successes of their followers as often as possible. Recognize, reward, and praise them frequently. Lead by example and by exhibiting your values. Consideration is the foundation of coaching. A manager must develop coaching skills to be effective in today's Information Age. When looking at solving complex problems, think "out-of-the-box." Search for root causes; don't just correct the symptom. When doing this always consider the employees working on the issues. If you keep the focus on always maintaining or enhancing your employee's self-esteem you will do fine.

Here are Seven Phrases that can help you show that you really care about your employees. Don't just tell them they are doing a good job ... be specific about what you observe. Praise can help you retain your employees if it's detailed and relevant. Start with these 7 powerful phrases:

"You've made my day because of ..."

"One of the things I enjoy most about you is ..."

" I'm impressed with ..."

"You can be proud of yourself for ..."

"You are doing an excellent job with ..."

"I was impressed with the way you handled the ... situation."

"You have really made a difference in this project/team by ..."

Try some of these and see the response. Consideration of your employee's self-esteem on this level has tremendous powers.

TRUSTWORTHY

Leaders must earn the trust of their people by doing what they say they will do and by being fair. They must create an environment that encourages each employee. If we look at the contrast between General George Armstrong Custer and Sitting Bull's leadership styles, as detailed in *The Genius of Sitting Bull—13 Heroic Strategies for Today's Business Leaders*, published by Prentice Hall, 1993 (ISBN: 0-13-349226-5), we might be less surprised with the outcome of Custer's final battle. I think we might find it interesting that Custer's actions the years and months prior to this disaster set the stage for his downfall. There are numerous reasons why Custer lost his life and that of his men at Little Big Horn. In fact, you could write a book on it and they did. I use this as a solid example of the need to develop trust among your followers. I will draw from a statement in the book (page 101), "Leaders cannot succeed unless their people trust that they hold their well being close to their hearts. Only then can a leader diagnose where they hurt and provide proper healing." I think this is a powerful statement about trust and its value to leaders. Your employees should be able to answers yes to these three simple questions about their leaders and the organization. It all starts with the person who they view as their direct leader. Chances are good that if they view the leadership as being trustworthy, the organization will also be considered a trusting place to work.

In short, if their followers can answer "yes" to the following questions, the leader is creating a safe environment:

Can I trust my leader?

Does my leader care about me?

Is my leader committed to excellence?

Creating a foundation of trust encourages commitment among the followers that will generate incredible loyalty towards the leader and the organization.

OPTIMISTIC

Leaders must provide a positive vision of the future. Develop a vision that guides your followers while allowing them to make decisions supporting that vision. Help your followers predict their future based on their own actions. Model the way with your positive attitude. Attitude is important for everyone and is critical to the leader.

If someone passing you in the hall says, "How do you feel today?" what would you say to him or her? If you didn't answer, "Great!" or "Couldn't be better!" then you missed your chance to positively impact the emotions of that person. As a leader, you're on stage every day. You must be real and believe what you say, because your followers will quickly pick up on the "real you" behind any act! Set the example with your actions. When people ask me that question, I say, "Great and I'm getting better!" Sometimes I'll say, "If I were any better, I'd think I were twins!" I've seen the difference this simple approach has on people. Your attitude is the control panel to your life.

This positive attitude translates into encouragement for your employees. Encouragement is oxygen for the soul. I have found, based on my coaching experience, that positive encouragement is ten times more powerful than focusing on the negative. In coaching my two oldest sons, I used to focus on the things they did wrong after a game and overlooked all the good things they had done in that game.

This was the same behavior I used at work during my period as a dictator. During my transition at work to a coach/facilitator, I developed a more positive approach. I started using this positive approach with my youngest son. My personal evaluation is that even though my two oldest sons had more natural talent, they never fully realized their potential. My youngest went on to be very successful in the sports world and received a scholarship. To this day he seeks my counsel on important issues. I don't have the same relationship with the older ones and I contribute it to my lack of support (encouragement) during certain periods in their lives.

I attribute a certain amount of this outcome to the way I coached my youngest son with nothing but positive reinforcement. After a game I always talked about what he did that was good. He would always know the things he did poorly and we would discuss them. This approach has also been very productive in my training classes and as a manager. If you look at today's literature you will see various programs on rewards and recognition being recommended. This is just another dimension of the need to encourage employees (positive coaching in my mind). Most employees can identify their problems when the conversation is structured properly. The manager's role should be one of encouragement highlighting strengths. This is a big part of being optimistic and encouraging your employees. This will create a work environment that the employees will value over money. The added plus will be they will value discussing issues with you because you have created a safe environment for the employees.

RESOURCEFUL

Leaders should provide the required training to assure that their followers are prepared for their jobs and responsibilities. Encourage collective intelligence and working with others. Break down any perceived walls within your organization. Being resourceful can be almost anything in the context of getting things done. Don't take no for an answer. View any failure as a learning event. There is no failure...only a learning outcome. Combining Resourcefulness with these others qualities will provide you with the fuel to accomplish anything you set your minds to. If you think you can you are right ... if you think you can't you're also right. It is up to you to choose.

I am particularly proud of the fact that we were recognized by the "Work In America Institute" in 1990 as being a leader in America for creating a positive work environment. We were awarded the "Leadership Excellence Award" for helping America change the way it works, through team development, training and innovative goal sharing. This award is a reflection of the change of our company from one that was considered a sweatshop in the 80's to a model for others in the 90's. We have had over 150 companies from around the world benchmark what we have done with team development. The foundation of this drastic change was the leadership focus on the five leadership qualities and a structured approach to creating self-directed work teams (Reference *The Trainers Role in the Transition to SDWT*, published by ASTD, author Ed Rose). The leadership at Intersil focused on making a major management change from a traditional management philosophy to a team-based culture because it was good for the business. They were successful and have been recognized in different ways for their success. The major side benefit for creating this type of environment is employee retention. The latest employee morale survey revealed the highest morale in 28 years.

During the month I was preparing this chapter, one of my key employees came to my office and told me he had just received another offer. Another company had offered him such a large amount of money that I said, "Well, I guess we better start looking for a replacement." His answer at this point both shocked me and made me realize that what I had been writing about really does work. He said, "Ed, money isn't everything. I like working here and I like working for you." Now, I really had to laugh at that thinking how far I had come from a dictator to a facilitator. Now I had confirmation I really was living what I was preaching. Well, I started to discuss the issue with this employee. Even though we couldn't come close to the offer the other company made, we were able to keep our key employee because of the work environment that allowed him to grow in other ways, which was more than just financial. This example couldn't have come at a better moment. Clear proof of the value of the ACTOR qualities.

If you, as a leader in your organization, embrace these simple but powerful qualities, you can develop a personal set of behaviors that will not only benefit you in your work life but, help you develop a better relationship with other important people in your personal life. Retention in today's job market is critical to a company's future. With benefits and other employee perks, it will come down to how they like working at the company. Developing a participative environment that allows freedom of expression and personal growth for employees will give you a competitive edge in retaining your key employees. The ACTOR qualities give you a foundation for creating and exceptional environment that will allow managers to build a positive relationship with employees. Remember, in today's team-based culture, everyone is a leader at some point in time, either at work or in a local civic group, church, etc. These qualities can and should be encouraged throughout the organization and used in your personal life.

THE LOYALTY EQUATION

Loyal Employees = Loyal Customers

by Teri Yanovitch

OVERVIEW

Given the rapid pace of change over the past five years—the mergers, acquisitions, rightsizings, downsizings, layoffs, start-ups and aggressive efforts to "steal" employees—it seems kind of quaint to talk about loyalty. But when thinking strategic retention, loyalty is often a win/win/win situation. It is a win for the employee, a win for the customer, and a win for the company who shows the loyalty. In this chapter Teri Yanovitch provides evidence for the proposition that a good retention strategy can be founded on company/employee loyalty.

INTRODUCTION

Most managers know what they want for their organizations: less hassles, greater productivity, being part of something positive, the feeling of accomplishment, and recognition. The list goes on. The question is how do we achieve what we want? Since the earliest of days, whether we were hunting for food or gathering for dinner, we have worked with goals and objectives, some of which we have set for ourselves, some which have been given to us. Some of which were written down, some of which were "carried down."

As managers in organizations, the major asset we have to achieve our goals is people. How we manage our assets will determine how successful we will be. Throughout history in the building of pyramids, in the marching off to conquer unknown lands, or in today's management of the most efficient department in a large company or organization, how people are handled plays a dominant role.

The ability to get others to do what we want is the basis for success. While pay is a perfunctory motivator we quickly learn that pay is not enough, leadership is required. That is why we marvel at special leaders such as Alexander the Great who motivated 50,000 men to march 10,000 miles on foot, into country they did not even know existed, and attack 750,000 or more heavily armed troops. What creates such loyal followers?

As we quickly learn with children, threats and other negative reinforcement only work for basic performance. Watching our professional athletes reminds us constantly that pay is a poor motivator. We see countless lucrative contracts given to high draft choices and free agents with dismal performance results to follow. For high achievement, other motivators are required.

The key to retention and one of the greatest motivators for everyone, is being part of something special, something successful. Legendary football coach Vince Lombardi was renowned for being a strict disciplinarian, yet his players loved and played their hearts out for him because he made them feel part of something special, they were champions in his eyes. Alexander's troops were challenged like few other armies, death was a daily occurrence; yet Alexander made them feel elite; he called them the Immortals. We continually see some athletes forsaking major financial rewards to play on a championship team. Everyone wants to be a winner. As good leaders we need to make our employees winners. All good leaders know the age-old saying "success builds success". To attract and retain good employees you need to build a winning team.

THE LOYALTY SUCCESS CYCLE

In today's environment, superior quality and service is the key. From the GAO studies to management gurus, we have learned that competing on price alone is often a formula for disaster. Long-term successful organizations have learned that increased margins and market share generated by providing superior quality and service generate a **LOYALTY SUCCESS CYCLE**.

QUALITY PRODUCTS AND SERVICE is where it all starts. Has this ever happened to you? You've taken your car in to be repaired and the service department is extremely friendly and helpful, your car is done on time; yet, as you drive off the lot, it is obvious the vehicle is not repaired properly. Or, the reverse situation, your vehicle is totally repaired, but the treatment you received from the service department was way below expectations. Their manner was condescending, you had to wait, the billing was wrong, etc...

Loyalty begins by giving the customer what you promised. It begins by talking to the customer to identify their wants and needs. "Quality is conformance to requirements" states Philip B. Crosby, author of *Quality is Free* and Dr. Joseph Juran defined quality as "fitness for use." Both are saying basically the same thing, meaning the product or service should meet both the supplier and customer agreed upon up front. For example, if you were at a fine dining restaurant for a special occasion, your requirements might be as follows:

Quiet atmosphere

Hot, gourmet food

Spaced timing of courses

Pleasant music

Courteous, respectful servers

You would not be a happy customer if the salad arrived two minutes after the soup because one of your requirements was spaced timing of courses.

This is what creates, **Loyal Customers** — the next stage in the Loyalty Success Cycle. Loyal customers are those who are dedicated, consistent and advocates for your business. These customers won't leave you for a minor price difference or a mistake here and there, because they trust in you for the long haul. They have built a relationship and an emotional connection between themselves and your organization. Loyal customers are passionate about your business and will sell it for you. They are also your best repeat customers, which leads us to the next stage in the cycle.

Repeat customers generate **Increased Market Share**. Typically 10 to 30% of an organization's customers leave every year. It is not usually noticed, because most businesses are working so hard to bring in new customers. These new customer sales mask the departing of the old customers. It is much harder to bring in new customers and in fact, costs 5 to 7 times more than keeping an old one.

According to Frederick Reicheld, author of *The Loyalty Effect*, if an organization can keep an additional 5% of their current customer base, they can increase their profits 25 to 85%. This leads us to the next stage of the **Loyalty Success Cycle** — Increased Profits. Based on Reicheld's research, a business can increase their profits up to 85% by retaining only 5% more of their current customers. How can that be? Repeat customers don't need advertising to bring them in to try the organization's products or services, they usually don't require as much effort, and they will sell your business for you. And if you're in a not-for-profit organization, those extra funds just mean more opportunities for the group you are helping.

When an organization is doing well financially and has happy satisfied customers, the employees benefit too. As part of a winning team, if they are given recognition for their role in creating quality products and service — morale increases. This, then, is the next stage of the **Loyalty Success Cycle** — Increased Employee Morale. Morale is contagious and can affect attitudes, behaviors, and the spirit of the organization. Bad morale can bring an organization down. Remember the downfall of Eastern Airlines? The final straw in that saga was the employee uprising against management because the employees felt unappreciated and ignored. The fall of Eastern Airlines, interestingly enough, has much in common with the fall of Mark Anthony (the Emperor, not the singer). The morale of Mark Anthony's troops had decreased to such a point that formerly loyal, dedicated soldiers defected to the opposing side — some even in the midst of the battle.

With high morale, though, in combination with quality products and services, the impossible becomes possible. Harley Davidson, a company once on the edge of bankruptcy realized if they were to stay in business, things had to change and change BIG. Management started listening to the employees as to where they were encountering obstacles in getting their jobs done right and where in the process they were failing to make a quality product.

Through a combination of change in management attitude, process changes, and employee involvement — Harley Davidson is an incredible success story today.

This takes us to the next stage on the Loyalty Success Cycle— **Loyal Employees**. Recently, I was staying at a resort hotel for vacation and one of the housekeepers smiled at me as I passed her in the hallway. Her name was Susan. In fact, I noticed Susan smiled at everyone who passed her while she was in the hallways restocking her cart. I decided to stop and talk to her. Bluntly, I asked why she was always so pleasant and friendly. Her reply, "because this is like my home and I want each and every guest to feel welcome in my home". Susan had made her place of work, a personal place. She treated the use of the cleaning supplies with the same thriftiness she would have in her home. She cleaned the guestrooms with the same care she would in her own home. Susan felt and acted like the owner of her assigned guestrooms. Susan was a loyal and dedicated employee. I asked Susan if she was offered would she go somewhere else to work as a housekeeper for $1 more per hour? Her reply "No, I'm given the tools and resources to do my job to the best of my ability here and I know I am appreciated. Management has weekly meetings with all employees and they ask us how they can be of help. We feel like we are a team working together to serve the guests. I enjoy coming to work everyday."

Are loyal employees more productive? You bet! When your employees are happy and satisfied, if they are nurtured by your listening to their ideas and given genuine recognition, they can increase productivity a hundredfold. Take the case of Jean, a data entry employee who averaged 560,000 punches per month when first measured. Recognized and shown appreciation by management, Jean set herself individual goals and increased them geometrically. After 6 months, Jean was averaging 3,526,000 punches in a month with no increase in errors!

And so the last stage of our **Loyalty Success Cycle** is Increased Productivity. Loyal employees tend to be long- term employees who have had the opportunity to learn the ropes, have more knowledge of the company's products/services, understand their internal politics, and are able to get things done quicker and better.

For example, a credit union was having a problem in one of its branches regarding its one and only printer. Members would sometimes have to wait as long as 30 minutes just to have a document printed. Different size papers often needed to be inserted depending on the type of document being printed and often documents were printed on the wrong papers. A group of knowledgeable employees got together and costed out the effects of these problems: $140,000. When they presented their facts to management it was easy to get the justification to add another printer to each branch location.

Loyal employees are also more productive when they see management's involvement. Alexander the Great got his soldiers to march halfway around the world on foot to conquer the known world. When he came across a fortress in India, they had been marching for seven years and were tired. The soldiers weren't very enthusiastic when Alexander suggested that they attempt to take over the fortress. One of the generals went to Alexander and told him he didn't think they could breach the walls that day. Upon hearing this Alexander immediately got on his horse, rode out to the fortress and pushed everyone out of the way and charged up the ladder himself followed only by his best friend Hephaestion. When he got to the top, he slayed all around him, then leapt off the top of the fortress wall into the midst of the enemy, where he and Hephaestion continued to do battle. Having done such, his own troops were shocked and mortified for his safety and began clamoring up the ladders. Unfortunately, so many climbed, that the ladder collapsed, trapping Alexander and his friend inside where Alexander was wounded. When the opposing army saw he was wounded, they immediately surrendered for fear of retribution they would get for harming him. They were convinced that Alexander was like no other man they'd seen before. Alexander's own troops were so upset, they went on a long string of victories to try and win his good graces back. The power of a leader's involvement!

SUCCESS BREEDS SUCCESS

When an organization is producing on-going quality products and services consistently and meeting customer demands whilst making a profit, we have come full circle in our Loyalty Success Cycle. "Success breeds success" and in our cycle, each element is dependent on the success of the other elements.

Where is the cycle most often broken? At the top — quality products and services. Following are two examples that typify the effects of this:

The first story is about Tom. Tom worked for a well-known pool decking company. Tom, the pool decker, was given the customer's address to confirm the colors and tile for the new deck. The customer was furious when Tom arrived at her home, complaining already of poor service received over the phone and upset over the delay in starting the deck. Unbeknownst to Tom, the company sales representative had promised the customer the deck would be completed before her Christmas party December 21, and it was already December 19. Tom did not have the available materials and manpower to complete the job in such a short time frame. Nor did he have the material and manpower to do the job till after January 1. Purchasing had saved all new orders for materials to the new year wanting to meet their budget targets.

For quality products and services to be produced, internal customer relationships must be explained and fostered with the same importance as external customer relationships. In the above situation, sales, production (Tom), and purchasing were all in conflict. The organization had set up an internal structure that created walls between the departments. Recognizing we are all customers and suppliers within an organization is a vital concept to communicate to all employees. In order to give our final customers what they were promised, all employees must work together with their internal suppliers and customers to ensure the final customer's requirements will be met. So many times, invisible walls are put up between employees and departments forcing conflicting goals and objectives.

SUPPLIER/CUSTOMER/SUPPLIER/CUSTOMER

The final customer seems to get what they were promised in spite of the organization — or they were just lucky!

Day to day frustrations, lack of ability and authority to produce quality work, internal co-worker conflicts and customer complaints cause anger, disappointment, unhappiness, and stress. When this occurs, the employee starts to look for a better place to work, thus turnover. What happened? The employee must have been happy when they came for the interview, the orientation, and probably the first couple of days on the job. Somewhere along the way, we lost them. And when we lose loyal employees, we lose loyal customers.

Such was the case in the second example, which tells the story of Becky. Becky loved going to the bagel shop down the street. She heard the bagels were better at the other bagel shop just a few blocks down from the one she went to, but Becky really didn't care. There were many things she like about "her" bagel shop: the small, cozy setting, the free newspapers in the corner, the help-yourself to coffee counter, but the best part of the bagel shop was Bert. Bert, the bagel maker and counter server, was a big guy and bald. Bert was a 20-year-old college student working part-time at the bagel shop for extra spending money. He liked the early morning hours, so his afternoons and evenings were free for classes and studying.

All the customers loved Bert. Whenever someone walked through the door he yelled out "Hellooooo there!" And if he had met you once before, he'd yell "Helloooo John..." When you got to the counter he'd tell you "what a fine day this was going to be" and "wasn't it a great day to be having a bagel". By the time Becky walked out of the shop, she would notice the lilt in her step and the extra boost of energy his enthusiasm evoked. Bert became a familiar face in a world of constant change and Bert paid individual attention to his customers to make each and everyone feel special.

But one day Bert graduated from college. He left his part-time job for a career position with a large firm in another town. The bagel shop just didn't seem the same. Oh sure, the small, cozy setting, the free newspapers in the corner, and the help-yourself coffee counter stayed the same — but a dynamic part was missing, the human element, Bert. Becky decided that maybe it was time to try the other bagel shop down the street...maybe the bagels were better.

Studies show there is a direct correlation between loyal employees and loyal customers.

DESERTION   AMBIVALENT   LOYAL

Loyal customers fall on the far-left side of the Loyalty Pendulum. On the far right side are those customers who desert you for whatever reason: poor service, rude employees, poor quality. As mentioned before 10 to 30% of an organization's customers leave on an annual basis. And they don't always tell you they are leaving; they just go away and don't come back.

In the middle, are the ambivalent customers. These are the most fickle, because they are indifferent and don't care too much where they go to get their products/services. Unless they are thoroughly delighted with you, they are most apt to leave due to price. Sixty-eight percent of an organization's customers leave due to poor quality and service. This doesn't leave too many left! Where we want our customers to be is on the far-right side of the pendulum – loyal customers. These are the customers who are dedicated to helping our organization be successful, consistent and passionate about our products and services. Loyal customers will not only sell our products/services through their referrals and advocacy; they also make up a majority of our profits. For example, United Airlines found 37% of their profit came from 6% of their most frequent flyers dubbed the Road Warriors. The blood banking industry knows 90% of the donations come from 10% of the population. An automobile model has a 63% repurchase rate, accounts for just 2% of the manufacturer's unit sales but delivers 1/3 of the corporation's operating profits.

What does this mean? You've got to keep trying to move your customers to the far right of the Loyalty Pendulum. Loyalty, quality, and service cannot be dictated; they must be earned. And when they are earned, pride develops. The customer is happy because they know they will get what they were promised, right, the first time, on time, and with a smile. Why the smile- because employees who work within such an environment are proud to work there and employees who are proud to work for a company, don't leave. In my next article, I will show how PRIDE can lower your turnover.

PRIDE GOETH BEFORE RETENTION

By Teri Yanovitch

OVERVIEW

If you have ever visited or worked in a company where the employees were proud of both their company and their role in the company, you understand the title of this chapter. Retention is dramatically increased, as Teri Yanovitch shows in this chapter, when all employees feel a sense of pride in what they do and what they have accomplished.

INTRODUCTION

Being part of a winning organization generates Pride. When employees feel pride in their work and their workplace, they are far more apt to stay. Let me share with you an acronym for PRIDE that touches the key elements that helps make employees proud.

P — PARTICIPATION
R — RESPONSIBLE
I — INDIVIDUAL
D — DEVELOPMENT
E — EXCELLENCE

Let's look at each one of these individually and relate them to employee retention.

PARTICIPATION

Studies going back more than a century show that the greater the participation and involvement by employees the better the performance. A sign from the early 70's found in an automobile manufacturing plant tells the story of management's attitude toward inviting participation from hourly employees. The sign read "Check your brains at the door before coming in and you can pick them up on your way out;" it became some cynical manager's way of saying — "we don't want you to think, that's our job." Perhaps it was fear that the hourly employee might know more than management knew or perhaps it was because of the feeling of power and control it gave to the manager. Whatever the reason, employees receiving this message certainly were not interested in participating in ways to improve processes. They did the job they were told to do; no more than that and less if they could get by with it, collected their paychecks, and put their thoughts and energies into outside work activities and interests.

Once companies began to change towards inviting more employee participation and involvement, they were astounded by the results. For example, an international design and consulting firm specializing in environmental engineering had a timesheet-billing problem. This was an area that affected engineers, technicians and administrative people because the timesheet documented how the workweek was spent and how the clients should be billed for that time. On average, 120 errors occurred per week at an annual cost of $30,000, consisting of time spent chasing down job numbers, express mailing late sheets, and re-keying corrected information. With the participation of the employees on how to correct this problem and implementing the changes, errors dropped from 120 per week to about 10 per week — a 90% drop!

RESPONSIBILITY

When you are in charge, you take responsibility. When everyone is responsible, no one is responsible. Aristotle once wrote, "When everyone owns everything no one will take care of anything." My daughter is 13 years old. When I am at home, I make her lunches for school, check 3 times to make sure she has her PE clothes ready, fix her breakfast, and continually remind her of the clock and the need to move faster in order to be on time. I am sure she could not be ready to head out the door at 7:30 every morning if not for me doing these things. Yet, somehow on those days that I am traveling and out-of-town, all these things do get done and she has never received a tardy slip. How can that be? Because she knows she's responsible when I am gone. I have transferred over that power to her! And she's proud to tell me how she managed her resources and time to ensure her deadline was met. Giving employees the responsibility and holding them accountable is like giving a set of car keys to the new driver. It is a sense of freedom, scary at times, but overall, a wonderful opportunity to show their skills and abilities to accomplish goals and tasks. Responsibility is a key factor in building pride—and people who feel pride in their work are less likely to leave a company. If you have ever been in a company where most of the employees are proud of what they do and their contribution to an overall goal, you will find few retention problems.

INDIVIDUAL

Many companies today are planning events at work to coordinate with families and spouses. Whether it is an Open House, company picnic, recognition ceremony, etc. more companies are realizing the importance of learning more about who their employees are, beyond the work job they were hired to do.

For example, the general manager of a 650 person mobile telephone repair plant spend the first two hours of his day just walking around to each work station and saying hello to every employee on the job and asking a question about themselves or their family. He considers these two hours an integral part of his workday. As you might imagine, turnover is not a major issue for this manager.

Relationships are stronger between management and employees when each knows the other on various levels. The manager who sees his lathe machine operator as the Little League coach in the evenings has more insight into the strengths and capabilities of this person. The manager who knows her steady MIS technician is a storyteller for the local library and volunteers' weekends to tell stories for Saturday morning children's groups, has more knowledge of possible career and development paths for this person. Knowing employees as individuals, their families, interests, outside talents, all are instrumental in building pride in your organization by fostering better relationships and/or by bringing these factors into the work place.

Another example of this occurred at Walt Disney World. In one of the back office warehouses there is a long white hallway to pass through to get to the stock. The employees (cast members as they are called) asked if they could do something with the boring, nondescript wall to brighten their working environment. One of the cast members with a talent for drawing offered to paint a mural on this wall. Management allowed the cast member time off to do the painting. He painted a splendid scenario of the four seasons and even included a hidden Mickey Mouse, which is a tradition of the professional Disney artists in the attractions they are consigned to do. This tradition involves cleverly painting in a figure of Mickey Mouse somewhere into the background murals and having guests search to find it. The cast members in the area were very proud of the mural painted by one of their own and anxiously invited their "guests" coming into the warehouse to look for the hidden Mickey. The individual cast member obviously felt appreciated and special for the recognition he received as the designer and artist of the mural.

DEVELOPMENT

A medium-sized manufacturing company began a formalized quality process and couldn't understand why two years later there still seemed to be major quality issues among front line employees. When asked by the account executive of the quality-consulting firm about the training of all employees in the quality classes, the Human Resources manager responded "Oh, we don't begin that training until they've been here at least 6 months!" Development of employees in understanding the culture of the organization, the expectations of quality and service standards, and the specifics of their job skills are basic to the foundation of their success. No wonder the company was still experiencing big quality problems. Employees need to begin learning techniques and tools to do their jobs right from the very start. How to handle customer complaints, service recovery methods and customer service skills are also vital to a new employee understanding and development within a job position.

Pride comes from mastering a level of skills and competencies and moving to the next level. Development of an employee does not necessarily mean moving to a higher position within the organization. Some employees are quite content to stay in one position, but want to develop within that role. For example, Mark is a chef at a large resort hotel in Orlando, Florida. Mark knows he has a choice of working at any of the resort hotels in this town of tourism, but Mark has been a chef at this particular resort for 6 years. Even when offered more money to transfer to a competing resort, Mark turns it down. Why? According to Mark, the resort has identified a development plan for each functional position. For example, within the food and beverage division, there are several levels an employee can progress through toward obtaining a senior position. It is based on job skills learned and effectiveness in the various levels. Mark has no desire to becoming a manager, but he is challenged by the opportunity to progress and move up within an area he enjoys.

The Nissan plant in Smyrna, Tennessee builds pride in its employees by paying individuals more for each new skill mastered. Employees are offered the opportunity to rotate jobs every two hours to keep the job interesting and to reduce human fatigue. The more skills mastered, the more variable the job rotations can become. *Study after study shows that the need to develop and grow is a key to employee retention.*

EXCELLENCE

Have you ever heard the phrases "just do the best you can" or "humans aren't perfect, so there will always be mistakes"? We have conditioned ourselves to say "that's close enough" and to accept compromises when it comes to accepting certain products and services. Companies have gotten by with this approach for many years now. But, today, as competition is becoming more global, the advent of new technologies, and more choices, customers are defecting when they are not totally pleased with the quality of the product/service and the way in which it was delivered.

There is no reason why employees should not be given a standard of excellence when performing their work. Do it right the first time – every time can be accomplished with planning and participation by the employees. Allowing deviation from this standard, allowing a "that's close enough" standard, is detrimental to the employee, organization, and customer. Excellence, giving the customer what was promised 100% of the time, should become the mantra of the company and anything less is not okay. It doesn't mean you will fire or discipline employees when errors are made, but it does mean you will find out what happened in the situation and see what can be done to ensure it doesn't happen again. Remember Eliza Doolittle, the poor peasant woman in the Broadway show and film, *My Fair Lady*. She becomes an experiment for Professor Higgins in determining if it is possible to change someone's environment combined with training, to become in this case — a lady. In the end when Professor Higgins is pleased to see that Eliza Doolittle has transformed herself into a beautiful lady with impeccable manners and changed accent, he takes all the credit for what he has done. But it is Eliza who tells him what really brought about the transformation it is "because you have treated me like a lady, I have become a lady".

When you provide a performance standard of excellence with your employees and expect them to meet that standard, in most cases it becomes a self-fulfilling prophecy. Alexander the Great as a child loved to hear Homer's classics—*The Iliad and the Odyssey*. He believed that he was a hero like Achilles and Hector and he lived his life as if he were. This became a self-fulfilling prophecy where his achievements were even greater than those in the legends!

What we know is that holding an employee to a standard of excellence increases employee pride and thereby increases retention.

THE PATH TO PRIDE

So what does it take to make the elements of PRIDE: participation, responsibility, individual, development, and excellence a part of the way an organization does the things they do? In order for PRIDE to inculcate itself in the organization, an environment must be created to support and foster pride. This comes from management taking the following three actions: developing the environment, leading by example, and involving employees. These actions must create and reinforce a culture that clearly spells out its values and beliefs, behaviors and expectations, as well as its heritage and traditions. Everything in the organization's environment speaks and it must speak a story of success. The above three actions are at the heart of creating this culture. Employees want to be on a winning team and it is up to top management to create enthusiasm for the vision of the organization, lead by example, and obtain their buy-in. If employees are encouraged and empowered they will not be looking to go elsewhere.

Taking a lesson from history as to how this happens, we can look at Hannibal. Hannibal was one of the greatest generals of his time. He wanted to build pride and communicate his vision of the power of sticking together in order to become the winning team. He called the army down to the center of the town plaza and asked for the strongest man to come forward. He then called forward his old wizened scribe. He asked for a young, fresh mare and an old mangy horse to be brought to the center as well. Hannibal bet the gathered army the old scribe could pull out the tail of the fresh young mare faster than the strongest man could pull out the tail of the mangy old horse. The army doubted such could be done. The contest began. The strong man pulled and tugged as hard as he could, but that old mangy horse just reared and kicked. The old scribe calmly and simply pulled on each hair of the tail of the young mare and slowly pulled them out one by one, winning the competition. The point being, if we all pull together individually as a team, we can win against even the biggest and strongest who work only as individuals.

Let's take a look in more detail at the above three actions:

Top Management Responsibility

Top management has the responsibility to define the type of organization it wants to be. Will it be reactive to the world or proactive? Will it be a leader in the industry or a follower? Will it foster respect and dignity among employees/customers or accept conflict and disrespect? Will it encourage excellence or be willing to accept less? Will it reward autocratic management styles or empowering and entrusting styles? If management does not define the type of culture it wants, the organization will define it for them.

Top management has the responsibility to set the tone through creating a vision and communicating that vision so clearly, everyone will know the direction of the organization. Top management must be able to see, taste, feel, and touch the vision themselves or they cannot pass it on with the passion necessary to drive the employees toward the picture. The vision should inspire and motivate everyone involved with a shared sense of purpose and meaning. Decision-making can be moved down the organization because the values and goals of the business are well known. Employee retention is increased when the employees' values and goals are in alignment with those of the organization. Having a common and focused direction allows the employee to move along his/her personal path of achievement, which in turn allows the organization to proceed forward in its path of achievement.

I know of a family-run timeshare company that had become quite successful. It had a major portion of the market share in the industry and was continuing its plans of growth and expansion into other parts of the country. As the company grew; however, the CEO was not able to keep up with the personal touch he had shown owners and employees in its developmental years. Front-line employees did not have the same passion towards the business as the earlier front-line employees had had when the CEO walked around talking to them and their owners on a daily basis. Turnover rates began creeping up, owners began canceling contracts, and potential buyers were harder to close. In an effort to bring the company back to its roots, the CEO was asked what did he want his organization to look like—yet he couldn't put it into words other than that as a comparison to a well-known world class organization in another industry. After spending a soul-searching day with the CEO and his executive team a vision was finally defined. The vision became a picture for all employees to use to guide their decision-making and roles. It was an image both internal and external for setting the tone in what this timeshare company wanted to be. The vision: " We fulfill our guests' dreams by providing a quality vacation experience that exceeds all expectations" was explained and communicated to every employee. Training was held for each individual within the company on how they could carry out the vision and it became a formalized part of the new employee orientation. Creating a culture does not happen overnight and all it once. Creating a culture is like building a cathedral, brick by brick, over time and envisioning the spirit and heart continually throughout its construction. Oh yes, the company made a dramatic comeback.

Leadership by Example

Leadership by example is what will cement the bricks of the culture as they are laid. Everyone watches the behaviors and actions of the leaders to see if they believe in what they say. A manager's actions are far more important than the words he or she speaks. If management says cleanliness in the facilities is of key importance and yet they walk by a piece of paper without picking it up – that action will speak far louder than any words. The manager who knowingly allows defective products to be shipped or the manager who knows customers are not treated well and doesn't do anything to change the situation is leading by example — and not a good one. There is a story about a lady riding on a sleeper train who finds bugs in her sleeper bed and after the trip writes a letter to the CEO complaining. The company customer service department writes a letter back to the woman expressing their empathy of the situation and apologizing for the bugs, vowing action is being taken to prevent this from ever happening again. The lady should be satisfied, right? Wrong, because in this case, the customer service employee writing the response letter forgot to take off the post-it note from the CEO that said "please send lady the bed bug letter." What kind of message does this send the employee? Obviously, the CEO doesn't really care if the customers are happy with the services or not. And more than likely, if the CEO isn't worried about customers being happy and satisfied, they aren't too worried about the employees' satisfaction and happiness either.

"Walk like you talk" is a dated cliché, but it truly must be remembered and displayed by management all the time. Alexander the Great wanted to promote respect among his troops and he showed this by his actions. One example occurred on the army's return home; Alexander decided to take the southern route and cut across the desert. Nobody had ever done this before, so they would send scouts running ahead to look for water. Alexander had been wounded in the last battle and was still suffering; now he had gone days without water. Finally, a runner came up to Alexander and said "Sire, they've found water ahead and we're so worried about you, we've brought you some." The soldier handed him a bowl of water. Whereupon Alexander poured it into the sand and said "I will go to the end of the line and only drink after all my men have."

Involving Employees

Involving employees is the third aspect in creating a culture that fosters pride. Many employees are afraid to get involved because if things go wrong, they might get blamed. What they don't think about though, is if they don't get involved and things go right, they won't get the credit either. Most employees pay for their own cars, handle rent or mortgage payments, buy food, run a family,and manage various schedules. Most know how to be efficient and meet budgets and schedules in their personal lives. Yet, on the job, employees are not usually asked for their opinion for a better way to do things or what ideas they may have. This decreases the employee's desire to get involved and management loses many opportunities for improvement in its products/services and delivery. This subtle message of "your opinion is not important" creates a sense of "unworthiness" inside employees, which often leads to turnover.

If the vision is communicated and explained so every employee understands how it relates to his job, service guidelines provided on how to achieve the vision, and a clear performance standard set for the expectation of excellence, the employee should be able to identify how he fits into the organization and the value he can bring through his involvement. Recognition of the involvement is vital to promoting employees to take the risks of sharing thoughts and ideas. Trust must be developed among the work groups and departments. Those organizations that have developed the walls between departments need to look at what it will take to tear the walls down. Communication between functions will help all employees see the bigger picture and have more knowledge to submit better ideas. Employee involvement creates a dynamic organization that can be ready for the changes the world brings and better able to handle both negative and positive events. Most importantly it makes employees want to stay with the organization and when employees feel they are truly contributing to the success of the organization, they feel a commitment to stay and see the results of their contribution. **PRIDE WORKS.**

CUTTING THROUGH THE C.R.A.P.

*Helping You and Your Employees Stay
Happy, Healthy and Productive*

By David Cox, Ph.D., ABPP

OVERVIEW

One of the themes of this book is that retention is typically an issue at "point of contact," that is, at the interaction of supervisor and the supervised. This article takes a different perspective. It suggests that many employees leave a company for imagined or embellished reasons that may have little basis in reality. As a manager this chapter can be a real help to you if you understand why some people leave and then, if they come to you before they have really made the commitment, you can help them "Cut through the C.R.A.P." and stay with the com-

pany. It may also help you as a manager to keep things in perspective as you work toward achieving goals.

INTRODUCTION

Retaining quality individuals in an organization entails recognizing that there is a multiplicity of factors that effect an individual's happiness, desire and willingness to stay with an organization. It is the responsibility of an effective manager to recognize the role that the organization plays in an individual's satisfaction as well as to recognize when the individual employee may be stuck with his/her own internal dilemma that precludes progress, stymies growth or manifests itself as the "desire to pursue other interests," Of course, there may well be times when an organization's orientation does not coincide with the interests of an individual employee and it is best to part ways — however we are dealing with the case of an organization *wanting* to keep an employee who may be looking for greener pastures. Hopefully, an organization can preclude such a loss by pro-active management.

US VERSUS THEM — THE INTERNAL AND EXTERNAL FACTORS OVER WHICH WE STRUGGLE

Over the course of my career as a psychologist, I have served in a variety of capacities ranging from management consultant to diagnostician to psychotherapist. In responding to a request to discuss what precludes progress in therapy and rehabilitation, I realized that for many, if not most, of my patients the same consistent issues have been significant obstacles to progress.

I have found that these issues are observed in a variety of settings, not just rehabilitation of persons with illness or injury, but also in the day-to-day activities of working and life in general.

Indeed, these issues are common obstacles in many, if not most, situations. From a psychological perspective, retaining quality employees is no different than helping individuals through the various difficulties that we all encounter at one point or another in life.

There are two basic types of obstacles in life. There are *external* obstacles and there are *internal* obstacles. These refer to obstacles that others such as government, policy or rule may dictate (External) and those obstacles that are generated entirely on our own (Internal).

These internal and external obstacles can preclude retaining productive, competitive and healthy employees. There are, in my experience, five obstacles — one external and four internal — that one must be aware of and overcome. Knowing what they are is simple — below I providing you an easy way to remember them — and once understood and recognized, they can help you maintain a stable and healthy workplace.

I like to use acronyms and other relatively simple methods for understanding more complex issues, when at all possible. Being the type of individual who likes (perhaps *needs*) to have relatively simple ways of understanding and remembering things, I have devised a two-word mnemonic device for these various obstacles. The first of the two words references external obstacles and the second word, actually an acronym, references those obstacles that are internally generated. The acronym may be slightly crass, however my work as a psychologist also tells me that fact may actually help us remember it! The mnemonic/acronym is

EXTERNAL C.R.A.P

The **External** portion of this refers to those aspects of life that are not under our individual control. The **CRAP** portion is the acronym that refers to the stages that most of us go through in problem solving and attempting to reach our goals. In remembering the five obstacles to productivity and progress, simply remember External as one and the letters of the word CRAP as representing each of the remaining four. *External,* C, R, A, P — five obstacles!

Before we begin discovering the details of External CRAP, a very brief bit of philosophy is in order. One of my favorite phrases, variously attributed to Spinoza, Descartes or Huxley, is essentially "Life isn't about what *happens* to us — it is about what we do with what happens to us." Another, probably a bit more well known saying/prayer goes something like this: "Help me to accept those things that I can not change, to change those things that I can, and to know the difference between the two." Both of these lines of thinking are essential to understanding and applying the External CRAP lessons.

In line with this type of philosophy, I believe that life is also about what we *make* happen. Your role as a manager in retaining quality employees is to facilitate in them a healthy response to the external and internal factors that can lead to reduced productivity, burnout, and/or turnover. You are responsible to help them see how that they can respond to what happens in a healthy, generative and productive fashion. If you are reading this and are an employee — and all of us are accountable to someone at some time, therefore we are "employee" types, at least — learn these lessons and recognize when these obstacles occur in your own life as well.

THOSE THINGS WE "CANNOT" CHANGE — THE EXTERNAL FACTORS

The first component of these obstacles, and the one over which we have the least control, is the External one. When I use the term "external" I am actually referring to processes such as rules, policies, laws and also other aspects of systems, bureaucracies and the various related red tape. It's easy to believe that the efforts that we as individuals put in get lost in the mass energy that is "policy", bureaucracies, legal or legislative systems and elsewhere. The whole process of organizational change, policy change, and winding our way through bureaucracy can be frustrating at best and emotionally devastating at worst. At times, we can put in our two cents worth, lobby and drum up support until the proverbial cows come home, yet feel no success because the specific goals that we desired were not achieved. However, we must realize that these processes take significant time and effort to change and seem often to take on a life of their own. This does not mean for us not to put effort into this area, as I believe quite the contrary is true, but it does mean realizing that despite our best efforts there are times when we will not achieve what we are intending to accomplish. When things that we cannot entirely control do not go our way we cannot, and should not, blame ourselves and become overly discouraged. "If it first you don't succeed..."

The *External* portion serves as a reminder that not everything is in our direct control. Nor are we, as individuals, the only ones who effect how we engage in the world. We are sometimes limited — to a greater or lesser degree — by the *External* environment. This may take the form of rules, regulations, laws, cultural mores, expectations, physical limitations and the like. External factors are typically not easily brought under the control of an individual. It is not truly that we cannot change those things, but rather that such change is often slow, difficult and not clearly related to our efforts. Therefore, it is easy to perceive those factors as things that we "cannot" change. External factors, when problematic in their extreme, are those that can lead to employee and/or organizational depression — a type of response to the environment at that psychologists know of as learned helplessness.

For the sake of demonstration, we will be paying visits throughout this chapter to a fictional character, Ralph. Ralph is involved in managing a company's shipping department, and his team was charged with responding to a large strike at a shipping company that was their major mode of delivery. When the strike was announced, Ralph responded by starting to calculate the late charges and lost revenues that would be charged back to his department. He became more and more depressed realizing that there would likely be many returns due to late delivery. He viewed this external event as crushing and out of his control — something that he "cannot" change.

When External Factors Lead to Internal Disaster

Dr. Martin Seligman, a psychologist working at Penn State, conducted experiments that taught us the concept of *learned helplessness*. I will briefly explain his experiment, at the risk of oversimplifying his research. A rat was placed in a cage that was divided into two sides. One side had a grid on the floor that could emit a small electric current — enough to be uncomfortable, but not enough for harm. The other side did not have this current. Between the two sides of the cage was a passageway that was either open or closed so that the rat could or could not go through to the non-electrified side of the cage. When the doorway was closed off, the rat learned that there was no escaping the electric current and eventually sat helplessly in the corner of the cage. Even when the doorway was then opened, the rat, having learned this helplessness, did not venture through the doorway. Despite a way out — the rat made no effort to escape the noxious stimulus of electric current. It had come to learn, in essence, that "Suffering through this electric current is a fact of life — I have met with no prior success and can not change it, so I will put no effort into trying to escape."

Learned helplessness can be experienced easily within organizations. Such an experience is often due to common external problems that employees deal with in an organization and can be categorized in two ways. One is *inertia*, the other is *instability*. These are a continuum, of course, in most organizations, with fluctuations and variation among people as well as departments or processes.

Inertia is an external factor that is a reluctance, hesitation or flat out unwillingness to change. The major problem here for a quality employee is that creativity and generative activity becomes stifled, or worse yet reprimanded. Employees are assets not only in their ability to perform certain functions, but also in their ability to enhance, improve and innovate. Generativity (defined as creative, original and productive thought and activity) is essential to not only keeping up with the competition, but to being there first. When inertia has settled into an organization, the company runs the risk of losing quality employees due to employees becoming frustrated with attempts to better the firm. Despite efforts to facilitate positive change through innovation or improvements, employees in an inert organization come to feel as though they are neglected, not perceived as important, and/or that the organization simply is no longer worth being associated with because the firm lacks the vision to follow up on constructive commentary from employees. In such cases, the grass not only looks greener elsewhere, it actually is! And the organization runs the risk of losing the grass roots!

Instability is another common external organizational problem that leads to employee turnover. Instability is the opposite end of the continuum from inertia — not only is there change, there begins to be a perception that nothing is constant, consistent or reliable. Instability is the antithesis of predictability. When an organization changes so frequently so as to preclude the ability to perceive constant values, policy, action or the like then employees begin to feel very uneasy. If an employee does not have some ability to predict where a company is headed, then the employee has a decreased sense of security. In these situations, it is as though the organization is a ship afloat without a captain.

Somewhere between inertia and instability lies the company's "dynamic" and culture. We have all read about and experienced corporate culture. Corporate culture comes to be defined, in large part, from the manner in which an organization approaches the world on the inertia vs. instability continuum, and the morals, values and ethics that underlie such an approach. Keeping in mind that employees desire to be a part of the team that responds to the world, innovates and changes, mandates keeping tabs on how the organization as a whole behaves. Quality employees do not care to be a part of a corporate culture that they perceive as either stagnant or inherently unstable.

Morale will sink like a lead brick when the corporate culture moves too far to either extremes of this continuum.

CHANGING THOSE THINGS THAT WE CAN — CUTTING THROUGH THE INTERNAL C.R.A.P.

For most of us, we know all too well when we are in situations that include external factors that we "cannot" change. We seem to have difficulty, however, recognizing in ourselves those *internal* factors that stymie our own progress. We get stuck "in our own C.R.A.P.!" C.R.A.P. is indeed what we deal with, or I should say what we don't deal with — for it is not dealing with the C.R.A.P. that leads to most of our difficulties in life.

THE FOUR INTERNAL FACTORS

C.R.A.P. stands for the four problems we humans allow ourselves to waddle in — *Catastrophizing, Rationalizing, Agonizing and Procrastinating*. Each of these are faced at one time or another by all of us. We use them in our efforts to avoid the difficulties of life and each leaves us as inert and/or unstable as the worst organization can ever be. As individuals, we struggle with our own sense of systemic balance, and don't always like to engage in the action of change that leads to healthy progress. However, if we can recognize these factors — the C.R.A.P. — that leave us stagnant or unstable, we can overcome them and evidence an evolution in our effectiveness in the world around us. Likewise, recognizing these issues in employees, and helping them overcome them, can lead management to a positively evolving workplace and significant increases in effectiveness and productivity.

CATASTROPHIZING

Simply Put —

The "This is the worst job/task/assignment/situation I have ever had to deal with..." syndrome.

The first of the four obstacles we have some significant control over is Catastrophizing. Making a catastrophe of a situation, if only in our own mind, may lead us to self pity, irrational belief about the situation and presence or absence of alternative possibilities, and paralyze us from going further with efforts toward growth and positive change.

We've all faced what we thought were catastrophes. These may have been job assignments, financial dilemmas, relationship issues or even something as "simple" as a passing flu or cold. If in our mind, we make the issue larger than life, giving it greater power in our lives than it actually deserves, we are catastrophizing. Somehow we feel overwhelmed and helpless in these situations, not recognizing the resources that we have at our disposal to overcome the problem. Perhaps we have made the problem so large — in our own minds, of course — that we feel that even the best of our tools and abilities can not help us.

Remember Ralph? Ralph was devastated by the news of the delivery company strike. There was nothing he could do about it and he could not change the strike. He started calculating his company's losses and started becoming more and more depressed. He began to look and feel helpless — like one of Dr. Seligman's rats! He catastrophized this event to the point that he was stuck in that mode. He was virtually unable to see any way out, and it wasn't until a loading dock employee urged him to remember that another firm had been calling looking for business that Ralph contemplated this as anything but a catastrophe.

Rebounding from a "catastrophe" requires recognizing that the situation is a temporary one that, although it may be devastating and discouraging, can change with time, effort and will. Most of us can generally recognize that what may initially be viewed as a catastrophe can be viewed very differently if one realizes the alternative, yet worse, situations in which we might find ourselves. These situations are challenges and may merely need to be overcome — or they may actually be the impetus for profound and lasting change.

Many of us believe that we can look for the "silver lining" of a bad situation and actually have good come from it. The "power of positive thinking" has many fans, and there is a reason that such a mentality persists. Other coping mechanisms or belief systems such as one's faith, can provide hope when we feel incompetent to proceed. The ability of survivors of severe trauma, concentration camps, natural disasters and the like teach us that there are truly few, if any, catastrophes that absolutely cannot be overcome. Ralph's situation was surely minor relative to many of those!

RATIONALIZING

Simply Put —

The "I did (or did not) do this because_____(fill in a "logical" explanation)" syndrome.

Our society places a premium on rational and logical thought. So why, then, is rationalizing a problem? Shouldn't we be working toward rationalizing our actions?

Rational thinking is certainly of value. But rationalizing, in the sense in which I am using it, is actually a psychological mechanism that makes us *think* we have done or are doing the right thing, yet we may actually *feel* that we are not. We give way to the logic of rationalization, even when we may *feel* that the logic provides the wrong answer. Rationalizing, then, becomes a way of explaining our mistakes or inactions. It can be a way of convincing ourselves that we are correct in our action or inaction despite the feeling that we are wrong. It is logical thought misused. Often we "know", in our heart or gut, that the logical rationalization is nothing but a way of explaining away a wrong. A reasonable way of recognizing rationalization in action is to note how much explanation something takes. To put it to rhyme, just remember "If it requires too much explanation, it's probably no more than rationalization!"

Ralph, our shipping department manager, made it out of the catastrophizing phase thanks to the loading dock employee! Unfortunately, he simply couldn't see his way clear to pick up the phone and call the other shipping firms. His company had dealt exclusively with the striking shipper for years — even decades! What would upper management think if he responded by going "out of contract" to deal with another firm? He was quick to *rationalize* his inaction — his inertia. He told himself and others that if he went with another shipper upper management would respond unfavorably, that he would be reprimanded for contracting with "unapproved" suppliers, and that the company's clients would understand the shipping delays anyway because most all companies were suffering as a result of the shipping strike. It was widely recognized that this shipping strike was going to slow down the entire economy! Rational thought kept him from feeling as though he were stuck in a catastrophe, yet it also kept him from responding with positive change to overcome the situation!

Rationalization seemingly gives us the freedom to logically understand why we are where we are, why we are not where we would rather like to be, and allows us to have discussions detached at times from emotion. For many of us, this is a secure place — the realm of theory, logic and presumed understanding. Rational thinking, of course, is something that we are all very good at. Unfortunately, this can lead to unending discussions and debates, that at times are quite refreshing and interesting, yet may stagnate, or even preclude, progress. Rational thought leads inevitably to various viewpoints, several of which can be reasonable and viable at the same time. Thus...,

AGONIZING

Simply Put —

The "I can't decide whether to A or B or C or...." syndrome.

Ralph's dilemma about shipping and delivery finally was beginning to catch up with him. He was getting calls from customers who were upset that they were not getting the products as promised. Yes, they said, they know there is a shipping strike at that large firm! Yes, they know everyone is behind in deliveries! But they didn't want to settle for that. They wanted, and needed, their product. Couldn't Ralph ship via another company or in another fashion? Ralph had to respond differently — he had to look at alternatives now. He knew that, but who should he contact? Should he contact just the firm that came looking for business a while back, or others also? And should he look to ship by land, as was the company's usual mode, or use air to make up for lost time? "This is agonizing" he thought.

Agonizing over difficult decisions, or perhaps even simple ones, leaves us in the never-never land of ambivalence and inaction. Oftentimes, we know that we must do something, yet in our agony, rationalization, and sense of catastrophe we are like a deer in the headlights of life. Immobilized by fear, anxiety, and other factors we stand still while the world passes us by. From a psychological perspective, I believe that this point of indecision and ambivalence is the absolutely worst place to be in life. When we are inert due to agonizing, we need to take action. Action is change. Many times, if not most times, this agony has to do with the anxiety of change itself. Change is difficult. We all know that. If it wasn't for that fact, many psychologists would be out of a job! Yet agonizing too long may also lead to further or continued problems.

Taking action allows us to engage in the most human of activities — learning. Without acting, we make neither errors nor correct responses. We remain emotionally and cognitively stagnant. We can not learn from inaction! We can (and hopefully do) learn from our mistakes. Therefore, it is imperative that action be taken in order to learn — even if the action turns out to initially be a mistake! The good news about getting off of our agonizing fence is that we can then begin to learn what actually needs to be done. We might even get it right the first time!

Sometimes we reach a conclusion and understand the need for action in the midst of our agonizing, yet we continue to fail to act. This can be because we recognize that the direction that we are headed in is one way, and we revert back to a prior stage of working through a problem — catastrophizing or rationalizing. At other times, we seem to accept the need to take a certain action, yet we still do not act. We move into the final phase of C.R.A.P.

PROCRASTINATION

Simply Put —

The "I'll get to it as soon as ..." syndrome.

Ralph received several reasonable proposals from alternate shipping contractors. He didn't sign any of the contracts right away, because he knew that the strike would end shortly. "I'll give it until Friday" he convinced himself and told others. "I'm wanting one more comparative proposal". "I need to finish off the month-end statement." You name it, he had a reason to put off his action until another time. Indeed, he was urged by many to sign with multiple shippers and get the product out of the warehouse, on to the roads and into the air. He actually knew what he would do when he took action, he simply was putting off taking the action. Perhaps things would change and he wouldn't have to do this...

Procrastination is something with which many of us are intimately familiar. In my last years of graduate school, as is true with many doctoral students, my house (including the outside of the second story windows) was never cleaner than during the time when I should have been working on my dissertation. My experience is that the living quarters of many graduate students are quite clean at dissertation time. Somehow we find other things to do even when we know what we really need to do and that it is time to act. Somehow, other activities appear to grow in their relevance and importance. It certainly seemed to become important to me to wash the windows, although that had never been a priority before! We procrastinate despite our awareness that we are doing exactly that.

I knew that I should be working on my dissertation. Yet the task seemed overwhelmingly large and I saw no end to it. I did see that I could clean that window though! And the window would be completed shortly! I was procrastinating completion of the dissertation due to the seeming immensity of the task. When I approached the dissertation a different way — breaking down the task into smaller sub-tasks, writing one portion at a time and rewarding myself with each section completed, I was able to effectively engage myself in the activity, working on it through to completion.

Similarly, there can be many reasons why an individual in an organization procrastinates. Feeling overwhelmed is one, but talking openly about the fact that procrastination is occurring, and working through the reasons why, can lead to an end of the C.R.A.P.!

WHAT TO DO WITH THIS INFORMATION

Calling the other firm, and two or three additional ones, Ralph negotiated contracts that remain in effect long after the strike — and that have minimized delivery time while actually reducing costs due to the competitive nature of the contracts. Ralph could have easily been stuck in catastrophe mode, responding to an external factor that he might have viewed as nothing short of devastating. He could have continued to rationalize his inaction, and let fear and anxiety overtake him, rationalizing away his role in the company's shipping problems. He could have agonized for even longer periods of time — having many choices can lead to a long decision time, can't it? And he certainly could have put off until tomorrow what he knew he needed to do today! We all know that one! But he made it — with a little help from his friends and his willingness to persist to overcome the C.R.A.P.!

The use of External C.R.A.P. as a way of understanding our dilemmas, and our responses to them, can help us improve our effectiveness, and that of our employees. Knowledge, like anything else, is worthless if it is not put to use. Actively using your knowledge and awareness of External C.R.A.P. is necessary if you actually want to overcome the C.R.A.P in your life and the lives of your employees and organization. Yes, even organizations go through the phases of External C.R.A.P.

Our limits are imposed largely by ourselves and may either broaden or limit our vision. The two-word mnemonic acronym used in this chapter is one way that you can use to understand yourself and others — apply it and diminish the limitations that are obstacles to progress!

So, if you catch yourself, employees or company stymied with a problem, remember:

It's not the External world that is causing your problems

CUT THE C.R.A.P.!

IS THAT YOUR FINAL QUESTION?

The Role of Compensation in Employee Retention

By Donald Sanders

OVERVIEW

Too often we see "experts" advocating of one of two extreme positions on the relationship between compensation and reten-tion. At one extreme is the notion that it is only how you treat people that matters; at the other extreme is the position that, if you would only pay enough, turnover would not be a prob-lem. These positions reflect the "Tyranny of the Or."

In fact, in order to reduce turnover, in order to implement a strategic retention plan, both how you manage and how you pay must be integral and integrated features of the plan. This chapter looks at compensation as a retention tool. It examines the three essential features of any compensation structure (base pay, variable pay and benefits) and shows how the three can be blended to increase the retention of key employees while not de-motivating others who also work within the system. Every organization should have its own strategic retention goals ranging from keeping everyone to keeping a select few. This chapter details the basics of how to design a customized compensation strategy that will meet your organization's retention goals.

INTRODUCTION

At the end of the hiring interview there is almost always a final question. Asked boldly or timidly depending on the individual and the position, it has to do with compensation. It is seldom as direct as "How much will I get paid?" but this is the implied message. The retention process should have begun long before this question was asked. Retention begins with a comprehensive system and compensation practices are part of that system. Before this question is asked, the answer should have been well defined.

There are few topics as daunting as compensation, when you link compensation and retention, the pool of Jell-O becomes incredibly thick. Yet, there are some approaches that we know are more effective than others, and some compensation tools that are available to many organizations that go un-used. The purpose of this chapter is to clarify some of the available options and show how they can be used to increase strategic retention.

The movement today is toward the strategic use of compensation and away from structured and limiting pay and salary grades, merit pay and performance review quota systems. Innovative compensation systems reflect and are a critical tool in the implementation of the organization's strategy. They recognize performance and financial results, stimulate innovation, discourage bureaucracy and ensure that the customer is a factor in how rewards are distributed. They are also designed to keep the best people while giving everyone a chance to share in the success of the company. Of equal importance, these innovative compensation systems don't put "golden handcuffs" on non-strategic long term employees who may feel unable to leave (and who probably should leave) because they cannot afford it financially.

One caveat before we begin. Remember that compensation can not be ignored as an important factor in retention, but not typically the critical factor. Manager to managed relationships, growth opportunities, career development and intangibles such as praise, pride and recognition are mentioned most often by employees in explaining why they stay or go.

WORKING IN THE SYSTEM

Having spent fifteen years improving systems via improvement teams and Statistical Process Control, it is difficult for me to look at compensation and retention without looking at a normal distribution. Remember that people work in a system that is established, implemented and maintained (consciously or unconsciously) by management. Thus, given a sufficient number of employees, let's say a minimum of fifty, you will find that in an average company the employees' performance can be viewed in terms of some approximation of the traditional "bell curve."

Thus, you will have about three to five percent who are outstanding performers, another ten to fifteen percent who are above average, but not outstanding, a third group of about thirty percent who are average to above, a fourth group of about thirty percent who are average to below average, a fifth group of about ten to fifteen percent who are well below average and the final group of about three to five percent who are marginal performers at best. This last group should be coached and counseled to improve, and, if they don't, should be terminated. Statistically, you will always have your lowest performers relative to your average and highest performers, but the goal of any compensation plan should be to encourage everyone's performance to improve. If the performance of the average employee is "X" today, compensation should encourage the employee to move to "X + 1" this quarter and "X + 2" the next.

APPLICATION

What does this mean for retention? Before that question is answered directly, let's look at the types compensation available to a company today. Compensation can be broken down into three basic categories:

Base Pay

Variable Pay (includes group variable pay, gainsharing, lump sum awards, and individual variable pay)

Benefits (Sometimes called Indirect Pay)

When you put these types of compensation together for any employee or group of employees, the goal should not be to simply provide someone a salary and benefits package, but to link the employee's interest with the success of the company and the satisfaction of the customer. In other words, the better the company does, the better the employee does. Compensation should be a critical piece of the puzzle in aligning employees with organizational goals. Research by Schuster and Zingheim on thirty eight "Fortune 100" companies as reported in their book *The New Pay* (Jossey-Bass, 1996—an excellent and highly recommended reference for companies seeking to understand advance strategies in compensation) suggest that companies who do so will have better (in many cases, significantly better):

- Earnings per share

- Return on shareholder equity

- Return on assets

- Profit margin

- Profit per employee, and

- Cash flow per employee

- And I would add, retention

Than those who don't.

So, how do you implement strategic retention through compensation?

BASE PAY

First, lets look at base pay. Base pay has traditionally been the measure of worth accorded to the individual by the company. The higher the base pay, the greater the worth. In old compensation systems, it was base pay that was often a determinant of who went with which company and how long they stayed. "I need another $ 10,000 per year" or "I was just offered $20,000 more by so and so to go to work for them—can you match it?" were frequently heard and unpleasant reminders of the importance of base pay. Base pay also impacted the balance sheet as fixed costs.

Innovative compensation systems look at base pay as a support structure for variable pay. Depending on the organization and industry, base pay might be established at the 50th percentile for that position in the industry. Again, depending on the potential of variable pay rewards (which could easily be equal to or greater than base pay), this might be set above or below this level. The important retention strategy implication here is that a high base pay

(75th or 80th percentile) may not serve as a way to retain people if innovative variable pay opportunities are being offered by competitors.

VARIABLE PAY

Variable pay is the critical ingredient in both innovative compensation systems and strategic employee retention. In many firms today variable pay is reaching to levels below executive to include not only managers and supervisors, but also professionals, support staff, and line workers. If your company is a moderately strong to very strong financial performer, it is likely that you will actually pay more in variable and base pay than you would have under the old system of just base pay—but of course this only continues as long as the company is doing well. Thus, the goal of variable pay is to directly link the performance of the company with the compensation of the individual. This process has been found to be a far greater performance motivator than an old fixed salary plan that included moderate to high benefits.

WHAT ARE SOME OF THE COMPONENTS OF VARIABLE PAY?

Group and Individual Variable Pay—The first decision that an organization needs to make is to determine whether the individual or the group is to be rewarded. Standard compensation systems focus more on the individual, innovative systems on the group. Within the group, of course, there can be individual differences where performance and contribution can be easily measured. If it can't remember the normal distribution and be careful of how rewards are distributed.

Profit Sharing—Again, this is of two types. There is the traditional deferred profit sharing paid as part of a retirement plan and the innovative use of a portion of the profits to be shared as an immediate and taxable reward for between 5 and 100 percent of employees.

Stock Options—These have traditionally been given to manager and executive level employees but are now seen as more widely available in some innovative companies. Because the employee is afforded the right to purchase stock in the future at an identified price, it encourages employees to work toward a better performing company. The drawback, of course, is that the market price is not always a reflection of value, effort or performance. Nevertheless, a comprehensive retention strategy should see stock options as an important element if the company is properly positioned.

Gainsharing—As the name implies, gainsharing is the practice of sharing gains that have occurred as a result of improvements in quality, productivity, efficiency and revenue generation. Gain sharing is typically given to groups who were critical to the improvement.

Special Awards—Typically a form of gainsharing, this rewards a particular group when a specific target has been achieved. This should be a forward looking award based on goals, rather than an after the fact award based on someone's opinion of the group performance. (Again, think of the normal distribution. When one group who worked hard is rewarded after the fact and another who perceives that they worked equally hard is not, special awards work as a demotivator for the second group.)

Bonuses—Executive and managerial bonuses have long been a staple of most company's pay plans. Today many companies have expanded these rewards to compensate outstanding performance by individuals at all levels. In my experience these efforts have done more harm them good. Of course a senior executive receiving a sizable bonus is likely to stay with the company. However, other's seeing this bonus, particularly a "huge" bonus, will wonder why they worked so hard to benefit this other individual.

Additionally, for managers and supervisors who receive bonuses, the bonuses quickly come to be seen as entitlements—something that "should" be received regardless of performance. This dramatically reduces the impact of giving bonuses on the very behaviors the company is trying to drive with the bonus.

Finally, individual awards often appear arbitrary to those who receive them (as well as those who don't). This is where knowledge of what I discussed earlier in this chapter regarding systemic processes and the normal distribution is important. Remember: people work in a system that is established and maintained by management. Without stringent criteria and a good measurement system it is very difficult to distinguish the A+ performer from the A or B+ performer. As it is with "Employee of the Month" programs, individual reward systems seldom achieve their desired purpose and often work as demotivators for those who don't receive them. They often do more harm than good in terms of an organization's retention efforts.

BENEFITS

As I wrote earlier in this book, (**Creating a Culture of Retention**) a good, sound, innovative strategic retention strategy includes some "differetiators." These are often seen as part of the benefits package. When you look at the array of benefits that are available today, it is easy both to see why they have generally gotten out of hand (benefits typically make up 37.5 % of payroll) and where they could be used to assist in your strategic retention plan.

What is meant by benefits? First there are health benefits such as health insurance and disability insurance. Second, there are retirement benefits such as pension, profit sharing (post employment) and 401 k. Third, there are benefits related to time when the employee does not work such as vacation, sick leave, and holidays. Fourth, there are a number of miscellaneous benefits that range from free day care to theatre tickets to company cars and company paid travel. The final benefits category relates to mandated benefits such as Worker's Compensation and Social Security.

With this vast array of options, it is no wonder that, in many companies benefits no longer serve to help achieve the goals of the organization. Further, if your benefit package is running at 40% of payroll, you have less flexibility with both base pay and your variable pay. Finally, your target audience for benefits must be educated in both the cost and value of these benefits. In one company where I was called in to consult, the company had actually increased turnover by offering hourly workers increased benefits in terms of their retirement package. The company had doubled the match percentage for the retirement plan, in effect giving the skilled workers they were trying to hold onto a significant raise. However, because the company failed to educate the workers about the real value of this benefit, some workers saw this "benefit increase" as an effort to avoid increasing base pay and they left the company.

COMPENSATION AND RETENTION

All of which leads us to an inescapable conclusion—to retain your best employees you need to re-think the what and why of compensation. If you are locked into high benefit costs, you have less flexibility with variable and base pay. Similarly, if you have high rates of base pay, you will have less flexibility with benefits and variable pay.

The key to designing a plan that links compensation and retention is primarily to be found in the areas of variable pay and differentiating benefits. If you are still competing for talent with only base pay, you are likely not going to be as successful as if you have a good mix of the three.

You cannot easily move from a structured and bureaucratic compensation system to one that is flexible and retention driven. To move from one towards the other essentially requires a re-engineering of the way the company looks at compensation. In order to make compensation part of your overall retention strategy (and it has to be), put together a cross functional team with an HR facilitator, learn about all the tools (types of compensation) that are available to you in order to improve your compensation policies, and then design a system to fit your company. In compensation there is no one best way. Mature industries may take one tack and younger, more aggressive companies another. Look at your company, your industry and become cutting edge. Once the plan is developed, educate, educate, educate. Take the plan to all employees and show them why the new plan is an improvement If they perceive that the company is taking something valuable away from them, turnover will increase. Remember your goals and the normal curve; use compensation to improve performance and to strategically retain your valued employees.

SUMMARY
Point of Contact

In many organizations retention is the issue that shouldn't be. We know what causes most people to leave their jobs and we know what to do about it. Further, we know that there is a direct correlation between how employees are treated and productivity, retention, customer satisfaction and, most importantly for the "bottom liners," profit. Retention is not a "soft issue," but a "hard one." It is quantifiable in bottom line dollars both in the cost to replace employees who have left a company and in the cost of lost performance. Retention is a critical business issue.

Today, many organizations are responding to unacceptable levels of turnover with the concept of strategic retention. Strategic retention, the idea that a company should identify the employees that it really wants to keep (this can range from 10% to 100%) and then implement plans programs and policies to ensure that these key employees stay with the company, is only maximally effective when there is a comprehensive, planned and consciously applied company wide initiative that involves managers and supervisors at all levels.

Which leads us to the question that is central to the ideas presented in this book. The question is this: "Is retention an organizational issue or an individual manager issue?" As I noted earlier in this book, that question assumes what Collins and Porras called in their book *Built to Last* (HarperCollins, 1994), "The Tyranny of the

Or." The question assumes that retention is the responsibility of only of the organization as a whole or only of the individual manager. In truth it is both. This is what I call the "Opportunity of the And." Retention is both an organizational and an individual manager issue—both are addressed in this book.

The three chapters that look at retention primarily (though not exclusively) on a organization-wide basis are **Building a Culture of Retention**, **The Loyalty Equation**, and **The Role of Compensation in Employee Retention**. All three of these chapters examine retention as an organizational issue. In **Building a Culture of Retention**, I suggest that, based on my experience working with companies to reduce turnover, there are eight steps an organization can take to pro-actively address employee retention. Among these are: commit to a retention strategy, provide defined opportunities for personal growth, demonstrate respect for all employees, measure the rate of turnover both as an organization and as a business unit, and add in fun and "differentiators." The chapter clearly demonstrates that, while recruiting and training are important, they are not, by themselves, sufficient strategies to reduce turnover and keep the employees you want to keep. Improved hiring processes are also important, but by themselves, are not a retention plan.

The Loyalty Equation by Teri Yanovitch takes a similar approach. She demonstrates how the "Loyalty Success Cycle"—beginning with the quality products and services that lead to increased market share, increased profitability and increased employee morale—is a proven approach to retaining not just the employees you want to keep, but the loyal customers who generate much of an organization's profitability.

And, of course, we cannot ignore money. In the third organizational-wide chapter, **Is That Your Final Question—The Role of Compensation in Employee Retention**, I suggest that innovative compensation strategies link productivity, customer satisfaction and retention. These innovative strategies use a combination of base pay, variable pay and benefits to say to the employees: "When the organization does well, we all do well; when the customer is satisfied and profits (or other measures in governmental services) increase, you will be rewarded." In fact, these approaches to compensation are a key retention strategy that are often difficult to establish, but once established dramatically improve such critical measures as earnings per share, profit margin, return on assets and employee retention.

You may have noted, however, that there are twelve chapters in this book. What about the other nine? These other nine focus on what is often the key determinant in whether an employee stays or leaves, in whether he or she is part of turnover or part of retention. This key determinant is what I call the *"Point of Contact."* The Point of Contact is the individual manager or supervisor. This manager or supervisor can be the CEO, the company president, a department or divisional manager, a line supervisor or a foreman.

The title is irrelevant, the reality is clear. In whatever position, by whatever title, *this person is most often responsible for the turnover that occurs within his or her direct reports.* Are there company-wide issues that cause people to leave despite the best efforts of the individual managers and supervisors? Of course there are. That is the reason for the marriage of organization-wide and individual manager initiatives in order to reduce turnover. Put both together and you can solve most of your retention issues, but for many employees the company is represented by their *point of contact*—their individual manager or supervisor.

Once or twice a year we see articles in major business magazines about the best companies to work for, or the companies with the lowest turnover in today's market. However, even within these companies, some departments, divisions or other business units perform better than others in terms of employee retention. Why? The "why" is the point of contact, the individual managers and supervisors within the company.

Thus the focus of the other nine articles in this book is on what the individual manager can do to increase the retention of valued employees. This fact cannot be stressed enough, if there is one critical meta-message from this book it is this: while both organizational and managerial initiatives must be taken to increase retention of critical employees, *it is more often the behavior of the individual manager, rather than the behavior of the company culture as a whole, that determines whether employees stay or go.*

Thus, in the second article, **Retention through Leadership** I provide a rationale and a blueprint for the manager who wants to become a leader that people want to work for. The research is clear. People value leaders who demonstrate admirable character traits (integrity, authenticity, courage of conviction) who are caring, who can communicate and coach and who have both positional and leadership competence. All of these can be learned and improved upon. If you would reduce turnover in your department, become a leader with these "Five C's."

In Carol Hacker's three practical and idea filled chapters, **Good Hiring Decisions**, **Recruiting and Retaining Gen X and Y Employees**, and **Giving Critical Feedback**, she suggests that managers need to see the uniqueness in all employees and to select the right people for the right position. Generation X and Generation Y employees are different in terms of values and beliefs from many of the "boomers" who preceded them. Managers need to be aware of these differences when working with Gen X and Y employees. Carol also establishes that feedback poorly given drives people away, while feedback given carefully and with a knowledge of the goal and the proper strategy helps people grow and develop—and as a result, helps retention.

Dr. Lew Losoncy, known for his work on encouraging employees, takes Carol's ideas to the next level. In his paradigm-breaking chapter, **The Soul Secret to Employee Retention**, Lew outlines the five basic needs of all employees. He suggests that, when the highest level of needs, those he calls "Inspirational and Insoulational needs," are met, turnover is reduced. At first reading this article may seem "far out" to some, but in re-reading, in looking at the paradox of "far-out" yet practical, the reader may find this just the right solution to turnover in his or her department. Why? Because if you can help your employees find satisfaction, joy and inner meaning in their jobs, they are not going to want to leave. As our world becomes more and more technical and more impersonal as a result, inspirational and insoulational management will become ever more important.

Dr. Losoncy has a "soul mate" in Dr. David Baker who takes the "Soul Secret" to the level of application in his contribution: **Bottom-Line Spiritual**. In this chapter David suggests that each manager needs to develop his own "philosophy of ministry," a grounding in the basic beliefs and values that drive the behavior of the individual manager towards his or her employees. We don't normally think of the "spiritual" (not to be confused with "religious") needs of the individual as having any real importance in the day to day work environment. But this notion is becoming more and more outdated as we find that the reasons people stay or leave have less to do with "concrete realities" such as benefits and more with "abstract realities" such as caring, challenge, enjoyment, a sense of belonging to something important and mutual respect. What we have heretofore considered least practical may be most practical in terms of retaining our best employees.

Talk about practical, Ed Rose has been there. In moving **From Dictator to Facilitator** as a front line supervisor, from the "baddest" to the best, Ed learned the lessons of how to keep critical employees. Ed has refined his method into what he calls the ACTOR strategy. That is, the effective manager is Adaptable, Considerate, Trustworthy, Optimistic and Resourceful. In his chapter Ed shows how to use this strategy not only to increase retention, but to become a model company. Interestingly you will find in Ed's chapter some experienced-based support for why Lew Losoncy's approach is so effective. (Ed Rose's **Reality Check—A 360° Approach to the ACTOR Strategy** is included as an appendix to the book.)

Further support for the "insoulational needs" of all employees is found in Teri Yanovich's second chapter: **Pride Goeth Before Retention**. In this chapter, Teri demonstrates that involving people, giving them responsibility, encouraging their individual development and striving for excellence, is a proven retention strategy. If you have ever visited a company or a department where there is a high degree of pride in both the individual and the organization, you know what an effective approach this is. When people are proud of what they do and proud of the organization they work for, they are far less likely to leave.

The next article, Dr. David Cox's **Cutting through the C.R.A.P.** is a resource article for managers in helping them to work with employees who don't seem to be achieving their goals and, as a result, are thinking about leaving the organization. (It is also a resource for managers who may be wondering why they are not achieving more both as individuals and as a department.) David effectively argues that people get stymied by five obstacles: the external environment and the four elements of C.R.A.P.: Catastrophizing, Rationalizing, Agonizing, and Procrastinating. If we can cut through the process, we can better achieve our goals as organizations and individuals.

Retain or Retrain? The purpose of this book is to show you that there is a choice, that there are practical strategies, day to day actions you can take, to increase retention and "retrain" fewer new employees. We know that turnover is an enormous, often unidentified, cost to organizations, managers and individuals themselves. Turnover doesn't have to be the issue that it is in most companies. By seizing the "opportunity of the and," with both organization-wide and individual managerial initiatives, with changes in the way we deal with the people we work with on a day to day basis, retention of key employees can be dramatically increased.

A closing thought. As I am making final edits to the text of this book on July 1, 2000, I have just finished reading the morning's paper in more detail than usual. Serendipity; in this morning's paper (the *Houston Chronicle*) there is an article buried in the business section on how Microsoft is moving from the use of large numbers of temporary staff to greater numbers of permanent workers. A quote within this story sums up in just two sentences what this book is all about.

The quote is from a former temporary worker at Microsoft who made over $80,000 in less than a year working for Microsoft's on-line division. Her quote:

> *"It (Microsoft) is a cash cow. I definitely got paid well, but when I left I took a job for substantially less money so I could feel more like I belonged on a team."*

There it was. Accidentally discovered, a quote used to fill a column's space that might just as easily have been thrown away. A quote squeezed between articles on "give away" items, problems with the new impotence drug and the signing of the new "e-signature" law. Yet it is a quote that should be framed and hung in the offices, cubicles and work areas of all managers and supervisors— by whatever title. It screams at us to re-examine retention strategies. It summarizes in 33 words the cause and solution for much of the turnover/retention problem. Managers ignore the message at their peril.

No doubt money is important, we must compensate people fairly and well, but it is the intangibles, the "insoulational" and non-material facets of being that provide meaning in life—and at work.

These are the consciously acknowledged and utilized resources of successful supervisors and managers; they are the opportunities available to the *"point of contact"* seeking to retain critical employees.

—**Don Sanders**

APPENDIX

360° Assessment

The ACTOR Approach

LEADERSHIP QUALITIES SURVEY

ACTOR

Adaptable

Consideration

Trustworthy

Optimistic

Resourceful

ADAPTABLE — QUICK SELF-CHECK

Indicate below whether you agree or disagree with the statements by circling the number below your choice
(Note: Read carefully because the scale changes)

	Strongly Disagree	Disagree	Neutral	Strongly Agree	Agree
I embrace change — it is a welcome part of my world.	1	2	3	4	5
I believe I have little control over the impact of most changes.	5	4	3	2	1
I feel anxious when faced with managing major changes at work.	5	4	3	2	1
I enjoy challenging old ways of doing things.	1	2	3	4	5
I exhibit a positive attitude when confronted with major changes.	1	2	3	4	5
I feel threatened and overwhelmed by changes in my life.	5	4	3	2	1
I am good at developing new solutions to new and old problems.	1	2	3	4	5

TOTAL _____

ACTOR — ASSESSMENT GRAPH — "SELF"

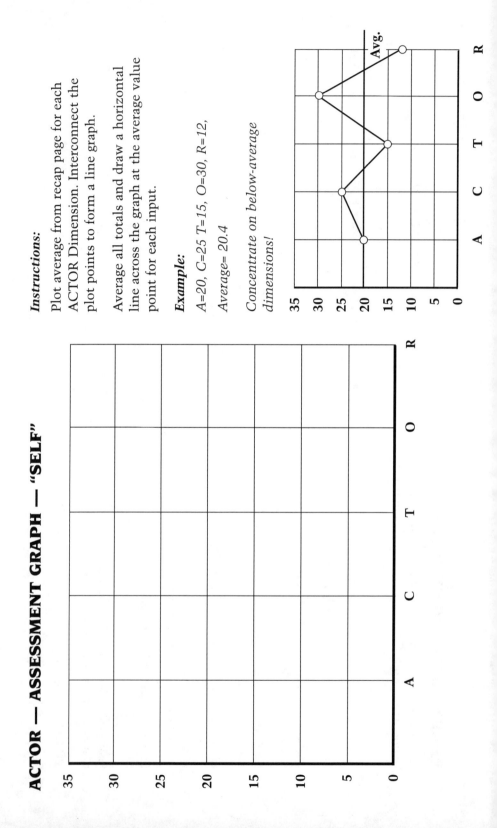

Instructions:

Plot average from recap page for each ACTOR Dimension. Interconnect the plot points to form a line graph.

Average all totals and draw a horizontal line across the graph at the average value point for each input.

Example:

A=20, C=25 T=15, O=30, R=12,

Average= 20.4

Concentrate on below-average dimensions!

LEADERSHIP QUALITIES SCORING SHEET

Adaptable:

30-35   *You perceive yourself as highly adaptable; a change master.*

25-29   *You perceive yourself as relatively adaptable; comfortable with change.*

22-24   *You perceive yourself as somewhat adaptable; may not have a high comfort level with change.*

16-21   *You perceive yourself as uncomfortable with change.*

Below 15   *You perceive yourself as quite uncomfortable with change.*

Consideration:

30-35   *You perceive yourself as highly considerate.*

25-29   *You perceive yourself as relatively considerate.*

22-24   *You perceive yourself as somewhat considerate; you may want to consider changes/improvements in this area.*

16-21   *You perceive yourself as relatively considerate; consider changes/improvements in this area.*

Below 15   *You perceive yourself as not considerate; this area may impact your ability to inspire and lead your employees. Consider changes/improvements in this area.*

Trustworthy:

30-35   *You perceive yourself as highly trustworthy.*

25-29   *You perceive yourself as relatively trustworthy.*

22-24   *You perceive yourself as somewhat trustworthy; this area may benefit from some attention.*

16-21   *You perceive yourself as relatively untrustworthy; area for development.*

Below 15   *You perceive yourself as very untrustworthy; area for development.*

Optimistic:

30-35   *You perceive yourself as highly optimistic and proactive.*

25-29   *You perceive yourself as relatively optimistic and proactive.*

22-24   *You perceive yourself as somewhat optimistic; this area may impact your ability to inspire and lead your employees.*

16-21   *You perceive yourself as relatively pessimistic; this area may impact your ability to inspire and lead your employees.*

Below 15   *You perceive yourself as very pessimistic and reactive; this area may impact your ability to inspire and lead your employees.*

Resourceful:

30-35   *You perceive yourself as highly resourceful.*

25-29   *You perceive yourself as relatively resourceful.*

22-24   *You perceive yourself as somewhat resourceful; this area may benefit from some attention.*

16-21   *You perceive yourself as not being terribly resourceful; area for development.*

Below 15   *You perceive yourself as not very resourceful; area for development.*

What are my strengths and weaknesses in this area: _____

What actions can I take to improve in this area? (KABS - Knowledge, Attitude, Behaviors, Skills) _____

INTERSILIAN [YOUR COMPANY] LEADERSHIP THOUGHTS

Team Members: _____

Adaptable: _____

Consideration: _____

Trustworthy: _____

Optimistic: _____

Resourceful: _____

REALITY CHECK

360 Degree Feedback

PERSON RECEIVING FEEDBACK

ACTOR

Adaptable

Consideration

Trustworthy

Optimistic

Resourceful

Your open and honest feedback will be value by the recipient

ADAPTABLE — REALITY CHECK

Indicate below whether you agree or disagree with the statements by circling the number below your choice (Note: Read carefully because the scale changes)

	Strongly Disagree	Disagree	Neutral	Strongly Agree	Agree
I embrace change — it is a welcome part of my world.	1	2	3	4	5
I believe I have little control over the impact of most changes	5	4	3	2	1
This person embraces change — it appears a welcome part of their world.	1	2	3	4	5
This person usually seems in control of changes in their life.	1	2	3	4	5
This person appears anxious when faced with managing major changes at work.	5	4	3	2	1
This person seems to enjoy challenging old ways of doing things.	1	2	3	4	5
This person generally exhibits a positive attitude when confronted with major changes.	1	2	3	4	5
This person appears to feel threatened and overwhelmed by changes in their life.	5	4	3	2	1
This person is always coming up with new solutions to new and old problems.	1	2	3	4	5

TOTAL _____

Please list a strength of this individual in this leadership quality: _____

CONSIDERATION — REALITY CHECK

Indicate below whether you agree or disagree with the statements by circling the number below your choice (Note: Read carefully because the scale changes)

	Strongly Disagree	Disagree	Neutral	Agree	Strongly Agree
This person consistently values the contributions of others by giving positive feedback/recognition.	1	2	3	4	5
This person shares info freely and often.	1	2	3	4	5
This person seeks first to understand and then to be understood, even when others disagree with them.	1	2	3	4	5
This person is good at listening and responding with empathy.	1	2	3	4	5
This person consistently maintains or enhances other's self esteem.	1	2	3	4	5
This person values other's inputs in problem solving, even if they appear to be way out there.	1	2	3	4	5
This person looks for new, creative, and unique ways to recognize & reward employees for their successes.	1	2	3	4	5

TOTAL _____

Please list a strength of this individual in this leadership quality: _____

TRUSTWORTHY — REALITY CHECK

Indicate below whether you agree or disagree with the statements by circling the number below your choice (Note: Read carefully because the scale changes)

	Strongly Disagree	Disagree	Neutral	Agree	Strongly Agree
This person is very open and honest with all team members.	1	2	3	4	5
This person shows people they care about them.	1	2	3	4	5
This person follows through on commitments in a timely manner.	1	2	3	4	5
People can usually count on this person's support.	1	2	3	4	5
This person is open to positive and constructive feedback from others.	1	2	3	4	5
When giving feedback this person generally gives positive & constructive feedback to others when it can help them develop.	1	2	3	4	5
This person creates an environment that values open communication.	1	2	3	4	5

TOTAL _____

Please list a strength of this individual in this leadership quality: _____

OPTIMISTIC — REALITY CHECK

Indicate below whether you agree or disagree with the statements by circling the number below your choice (Note: Read carefully because the scale changes)

	Strongly Disagree	Disagree	Neutral	Agree	Strongly Agree
This person is good at envisioning the future. This person develops long term plans that are communicated to others.	1	2	3	4	5
This person is very up beat which is obvious even when you ask, How are you today?	1	2	3	4	5
This person believes it is important to challenge existing paradigms in order to improve the business.	1	2	3	4	5
This person always appears optimistic about the company's future.	1	2	3	4	5
This person gives the perception that an individual can have very little impact in their organization.	5	4	3	2	1
This person is willing to take a step backwards at times so they can take two steps forward.	1	2	3	4	5
This person sees problems as opportunities to improve the situation.	1	2	3	4	5

TOTAL _____

Please list a strength of this individual in this leadership quality: _____

RESOURCEFUL — REALITY CHECK

Indicate below whether you agree or disagree with the statements by circling the number below your choice (Note: Read carefully because the scale changes)

	Strongly Disagree	Disagree	Neutral	Agree	Strongly Agree
This person is good at breaking down barriers to achieve goals.	1	2	3	4	5
This person works to establish good working relations with people outside their area in order to serve our customers better.	1	2	3	4	5
This person does not delegate; they would rather do it themselves — they micromanage.	5	4	3	2	1
This person is not usually open to new, untried ideas. They prefer things that have worked right in the past.	5	4	3	2	1
This person will take whatever action necessary to obtain resources so their team can get the job done, even when resources are scarce.	1	2	3	4	5
This person doesn't usually ask for help from anyone.	5	4	3	2	1
This person doesn't hesitate to recommend other resources when they may not have the technical or other expertise to solve the problem.	1	2	3	4	5

TOTAL _____

Please list a strength of this individual in this leadership quality: _____

REALITY CHECK LEADERSHIP QUALITIES SCORING SHEET

Adaptable:

30-35	Others perceive you as highly adaptable; a change master.
25-29	Others perceive you as relatively adaptable; comfortable with change.
22-24	Others perceive you as somewhat adaptable; may not have a high comfort level with change.
16-21	Others perceive you as uncomfortable with change.
Below 15	Others perceive you as quite uncomfortable with change.

Consideration:

30-35	Others perceive you as highly considerate.
25-29	Others perceive you as relatively considerate.
22-24	Others perceive you as somewhat considerate; you may want to consider changes/improvements in this area.
16-21	Others perceive you as relatively considerate; consider changes/improvements in this area.
Below 15	Others perceive you as not considerate; this area may impact your ability to inspire and lead your employees. Consider changes/improvements in this area.

Trustworthy:

30-35	Others perceive you as highly trustworthy.
25-29	Others perceive you as relatively trustworthy.
22-24	Others perceive you as somewhat trustworthy; this area may benefit from some attention.
16-21	Others perceive you as relatively untrustworthy; area for development.
Below 15	Others perceive you as very untrustworthy; area for development.

Optimistic:

30-35	Others perceive yourself as highly optimistic and proactive.
25-29	Others perceive yourself as relatively optimistic and proactive.
22-24	Others perceive yourself as somewhat optimistic; this area may impact your ability to inspire and lead your employees.
16-21	Others perceive yourself as relatively pessimistic; this area may impact your ability to inspire and lead your employees.
Below 15	Others perceive yourself as very pessimistic and reactive; this area may impact your ability to inspire and lead your employees.

Resourceful:

30-35	Others perceive yourself as highly resourceful.
25-29	Others perceive yourself as relatively resourceful.
22-24	Others perceive yourself as somewhat resourceful; this area may benefit from some attention.
16-21	Others perceive yourself as not being terribly resourceful; area for development.
Below 15	Others perceive yourself as not very resourceful; area for development.

Note: Most of us can recognize our weaknessees. Sometimes we don't notice our strengths because they are natural and we don't get told as much about them. Important to note, however, that sometimes an over-use of a strength can be a career limiting weakness.

What strengths do others perceive in you? (List): _____

ACTOR — ASSESSMENT GRAPH — "OTHER"

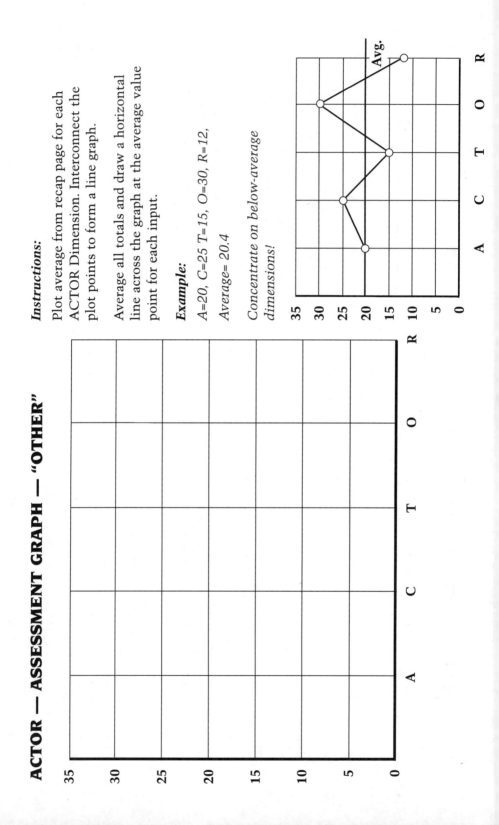

Instructions:

Plot average from recap page for each ACTOR Dimension. Interconnect the plot points to form a line graph.

Average all totals and draw a horizontal line across the graph at the average value point for each input.

Example:

A=20, C=25 T=15, O=30, R=12,

Average= 20.4

Concentrate on below-average dimensions!

ACTOR — REALITY CHECK

REALITY CHECK
RECAP PAGE

Person	A		C		T		O		R
A									
B									
C									
D									
Total Ave. (Round Up)									
Strengths									

INTERSILIAN [YOUR COMPANY] LEADERSHIP THOUGHTS

Team Members: Jeremy Flann, Hans-Peter Hoenes, Shalui Patel, Jacqueline DeGrave, Stephanie Jones

Adaptable: Look for new ways to change to stay ahead of the pack.

Consideration: Find new ways to nurture your team and take time to hear their views and ideas.

Trustworthy: Earn trust through consistent, ethical & loyal behavior.

Optimistic: Always project a positive attitude to the future.

Resourceful: Use information from all possible sources and look for new ways to meet challenges.

INTERSILIAN [YOUR COMPANY] LEADERSHIP THOUGHTS

Team Members: Phil, Uri, Peter, Roberto, Juergen

Adaptable: Change is inevitable, change is an opportunity, a good leader will adapt to, influence and encourage the change throughout the organization.

Consideration: Listen, understand, respect and value others, treat others as you would wish to be treated.

Trustworthy: Trust is earned by delivering upon your promises. Trust is the fuel of all relationships.

Optimistic: How do you feel? I feel great! Optimism is a key characteristic of a successful leader — use it.

Resourceful: Draw on those that are around you to facilitate success.

INTERSILIAN [YOUR COMPANY] LEADERSHIP THOUGHTS

Team Members: Tracy, Nic, MB, Craig (Green Team)

Adaptable: The world is continuously changing and the people must adapt to succeed in the company.

Consideration: Take the time to listen to peoples' views.

Trustworthy: Provide safe and open environment for open communication.

Optimistic: Pessimism will never inspire, optimist will always inspire.

Resourceful: Explore all the roads to none.

INTERSILIAN [YOUR COMPANY] LEADERSHIP THOUGHTS

Team Members: Lutier, Vannin, Wector, Whitehouse, Zanellatto

Adaptable: Seek out welcome and adapt to change.

Consideration: Remember that we are individual, belonging to one team.

Trustworthy: Creating an open and trustworthy environment.

Optimistic: Aim to bring sunshine into other's lives you will also gain a sun-tan.

Resourceful: The well traveled route may not always be the best.

CONSIDERATION — QUICK SELF-CHECK

Indicate below whether you agree or disagree with the statements by circling the number below your choice (Note: Read carefully because the scale changes)

	Strongly Disagree	Disagree	Neutral	Agree	Strongly Agree
I consistently value the contributions of others by giving positive feedback/recognition.	1	2	3	4	5
I share information freely and often.	1	2	3	4	5
I seek first to understand and then to be understood, even when others disagree with me.	1	2	3	4	5
I am good at listening and responding with empathy.	1	2	3	4	5
I consistently maintain or enhance other's self esteem.	1	2	3	4	5
I value other's inputs in problem solving, even if they appear to be way out there.	1	2	3	4	5
I look for new, creative, and unique ways to tailor rewards for employee successes.	1	2	3	4	5

TOTAL _____

TRUSTWORTHY — QUICK SELF-CHECK

Indicate below whether you agree or disagree with the statements by circling the number below your choice (Note: Read carefully because the scale changes)

	Strongly Disagree	Disagree	Neutral	Agree	Strongly Agree
I am open and honest with my team members.	1	2	3	4	5
I show people I care about them.	1	2	3	4	5
I follow through on commitments in a timely manner.	1	2	3	4	5
Team members can count on my support.	1	2	3	4	5
I am open to positive and constructive feedback from my team members.	1	2	3	4	5
I give positive and constructive feedback to my team when it can help them develop.	1	2	3	4	5
I strive to create an environment that values open communication.	1	2	3	4	5

TOTAL _____

OPTIMISTIC — QUICK SELF-CHECK

Indicate below whether you agree or disagree with the statements by circling the number below your choice (Note: Read carefully because the scale changes)

	Strongly Disagree	Disagree	Neutral	Agree	Strongly Agree
I take time to envision the future by periodically setting time aside for long-term planning.	1	2	3	4	5
I am very upbeat which is obvious when someone asks me, How are you today?	1	2	3	4	5
I believe it is important to challenge existing paradigms in order to improve our business.	1	2	3	4	5
I feel optimistic about the company's future.	1	2	3	4	5
In reality, an individual like me can have very little impact in my organization.	5	4	3	2	1
I believe sometimes it s okay to take a step backwards to we can take two steps forward.	1	2	3	4	5
I see most problems as opportunities to improve	1	2	3	4	5

TOTAL _____

RESOURCEFUL — QUICK SELF-CHECK

Indicate below whether you agree or disagree with the statements by circling the number below your choice (Note: Read carefully because the scale changes)

	Strongly Disagree	Disagree	Neutral	Agree	Strongly Agree
I am good at breaking down barriers to achieve goals.	1	2	3	4	5
I work to establish good working relations with people outside my area in order to serve our customers better.	1	2	3	4	5
If you want a job done right, you have to do it yourself.	5	4	3	2	1
My reaction to a new, untried idea is sometimes that will never work here.	5	4	3	2	1
I go out of my way to obtain needed inputs and resources so my team can get the job done, even when resources are scarce.	1	2	3	4	5
I ask for help when I can.	1	2	3	4	5
I don't hesitate to recommend other resources when I may not have the technical or other expertise to solve the problem.	1	2	3	4	5

TOTAL _____